How To Raise
A Cat
When
Nobody's Home

Training and Fun
For You and
The Family Cat

Written by Jerry Climer
Illustrated by Robert R. Hetzer
Cover Design by Robert R. Hetzer

Published by
Penny Dreadful Publishers
P.O. Box 364
Jackson, Michigan
49204

Set in Typeface designed for easy reading
Printed in the United States of America

International Standard Book Number 0-911793-01 1

Preface

Dear Readers,

In this book I have tried to share with you the joy and companionship our family has shared with our cats and the rewards of having well-trained, fun loving feline friends.

I designed the book to be read from cover to cover in just a few evenings. Along with training suggestions there are also stories to instruct and entertain you.

Once you have read this easy-to-use guide to successful cat rearing, you will wish to refer to it frequently as you encounter discipline problems with your growing kitten. In fact, the reason I am asking you to read the book through at once, is because many times the solutions given in one area of training, may also be used successfully in other situations.

I hope all of you from eight to eighty, enjoy raising a healthy, happy, loving cat to maturity and old age with the help of this book.

Jerry Climer

*This book was inspired by
and dedicated to my
children and their cats*

*Carrie and Simon
Kelly and Charlie
Paul and Judy with
Sammy and Baby
Lisa and Phil
with Ozzie
Linda and David and Twins
Shannon and Michelle
with Fozzie Bear*

*With appreciation to
Marian W. Koppler
Jaunita Riedel
David B. Shannon
Margery Duane
Lisa Climer-Harding*

TABLE OF CONTENTS

PART 1   HOW TO RAISE A CAT
          WHEN NOBODY'S HOME

PART 2   THE NOBODY'S HOME CAT GROWS UP

PART 3   PENNY PINCHING HOME HEALTH CARE

PART 4 MAN AND CAT
          LIVING, LOVING, COPING

PART 5 QUESTIONS AND ANSWERS

PART 1

How To Raise A Cat When Nobody's Home

CONVENIENT PETS FOR TODAY'S BUSY PEOPLE

Many young couples today share comfortable incomes which provide not only necessities, but a variety of luxuries as well. They have lots of friends and usually are involved in a variety of weekend social events. The parents of these young adults, now alone after years of child rearing, also want to feel free to participate in social and cultural activities and to travel without being tied down.

Though life for these childless families is good, there's still a desire for some loving companion to come home to. So what do they do? In the highly populated metropolitan areas, as well as in the suburbs, they lavish their money and affection on the cat, the easiest-to-care-for of all house pets.

Cat ownership has steadily expanded over the last two years with an increasing number of Americans deciding every day that felines are their kind of pet. Now more than ever before, because of our changing social trends, both mixed breed and pedigreed cats have the chance to live in the lap of luxury. Cat food captures a growing share of the retail market, and cat care supplies—dishes, climbing trees, toys, grooming aids, books—are a major market in a fluctuating national economy.

In large cities, it's common to find two-career families choosing cats as the most suitable companions for apartment living. If they desire a classy exotic breed, there is a large selection; and of course, mixed breeds are available at all animal shelters. Once neutered, the cats can be brought home and quickly litter-trained. The owners then have clean-living, attractive, loving companions waiting each evening for their return. Cats don't have to be walked. In fact, for their entire lives, they may never go out of doors except to visit the vet.

Cats are easily groomed, can cuddle up with you in bed; and best of all, cats may be occasionally left alone overnight since generous amounts of both dry and semi-moist foods can be safely left in the cat's dish. Given a good supply of water and a clean litter box, the kitty can do quite well by himself for a day or so. Of course, it's always comforting if a neighbor drops in to give the cat a little companionship.

Felines are so convenient to live with that a growing number of single men, once scorning cats with grim macho disdain, are now finding that the companionship of a cat relieves loneliness without altering their lifestyles.

While cats can be demanding and sometimes naughty, they require very little energy and care, compared to other household pets. In return they offer love and friendship. Their most endearing quality is their need for affection.

Cats make ideal playmates for children. They teach responsibility, are noncritical and happily greet the child coming into an empty home after school. Unlike the adults who control a child's life, cats don't give orders and require little attention.

GIVING A CAT AS A PRESENT

Along with America's changing patterns of living, customs of gift-giving vary according to the new lifestyle. Once considered irresponsible, giving a cat as a present is now considered a delightful and innovative surprise for adults living alone or with older children. Of course, any time a pet is given as a gift, the giver must be assured that the pet is wanted and will be cared for and loved. When

giving a cat as a gift, advance preparation is the key to success.

The gift of a cat must fit the owner's needs, and sometimes on-the-spot changes must be coped with. We learned a good lesson when we gave a cat to our oldest daughter. She was about 13 years old at the time and desperately wanted a Siamese kitten. On Christmas Day, because of the presence of younger children and all the excitement, Linda received a beautifully wrapped, stuffed Siamese cat with a note assuring her that we would take her to the cattery and allow her to select the kitten she liked best. After a few days of excited anticipation, we went to visit the kittens and allowed Linda to make her selection.

On seeing the litter, we immediately fell in love with each kitten that crawled over our laps and batted at our shoelaces. Linda, delighted with all, finally selected an adorable female kitten and we prepared to leave, giving the breeder repeated assurances that we would follow his instructions. As we opened the door, a half-grown, cross-eyed, male Siamese, shunned by all buyers, dashed into the room, talking all the way. Need I tell you that our daughter immediately changed her mind, opting to adopt the reject, named Charlie. We shared our lives and love with that mouthy, charming boy for more than 10 years.

We learned with our daughter that it's human nature to talk about pets we have always wanted, but our wishes can change in just a moment. If you are confident that a gift of a cat will be well received, giving a stuffed toy beforehand and allowing the receiver to make the final selection makes good sense.

Over the years I have often given a much desired cat as a gift by first presenting the stuffed animal on Christmas night, then when all the noise and excitement has abated, brought home the live kitten with the necessities for its care. However you decide to give it, a loving cat makes every home a little brighter and every heart a little warmer.

PETS—A FAMILY COMMITMENT

The decision to bring a new pet into your heart and home calls for a definite commitment by the family. Caring for a pet is a learning experience for your child but in reality everyone concerned must at times share in the responsibility. Whether you acquire a kitten or an older cat, all work involved should be delegated among family members.

Consider these questions before your family makes the selection. Do you plan to raise an indoor/outdoor cat, or will you keep him confined inside all of the time? Would you enjoy a long haired kitten? They are beautiful, but require many hours of brushing. If you teach your kitten to enjoy being groomed while he is young, you may find fussing over him in the evening while you watch television allows you to do three activities at once. You will keep your hands busy, which most people like to do; you will enjoy your favorite T.V. show and you will share attention and affection with your cat. Do not expect a child to take complete care of a long-haired cat's grooming needs. Everyone in the family, at one time or another should help.

Certainly few cat owners would allow a valuable pedigreed cat to roam outside and possibly get injured or stolen, and statistics prove that indoor cats live longer since they are continually cared for and protected.

It is easy to decide that your small kitten will never be allowed outside but when you take a stray cat into your family, many times this decision is made by the cat, who will yell for days if not allowed outside. This is often frustrating for the patient owners and most of the time both cat and his new family will be happier when the stray is allowed to establish his/her own routine. It is a comfort to remember that your cat knows how to survive outside.

BRINGING UP BABY

When you bring a new kitten into your home, all responsibility for protection and development instantly shifts from the mother cat to you. While raising her family, the mother cat nipped, patted and growled at her kittens to teach them proper behavior. It will be necessary for you to continue a similar parental pattern if you wish to raise a loving, well-behaved kitten.

Since cats are creatures of habit and enjoy living in an orderly environment, it is not difficult to establish proper behavior if training begins early and is consistent. The feline brain develops just as rapidly as the feline body; the kitten's physical and intellectual growth are nearly complete by the time he is five or six months old. With this in mind, it's easy to see why early training is so important. Most of your training should be done before the cat is six months old. The habits of an older cat can be changed, but why wait? It will be much harder on both you and the cat.

Cats are independent and dependent at the same time. They are also the most social and antisocial of all household pets—and the bossiest and lovingest of all animals.

These contradictory characteristics are one of the reasons we love our cats. We do not want nor would they allow us to destroy or alter these traits in the training process. All kitten training should be done with gentle discipline and lots of love.

Before you bring a kitten into your home, set aside a small area, cage or room in which to isolate the kitten when you cannot or do not wish to watch him. This will keep him out of mischief, and prevent the development of bad habits when he is left alone. Ideally, it should be in a light, airy room with a window through which the kitten can view the world. If you have a small laundry or bathroom, it can easily be made cat-proof and safe for the kitten. It does provide more stretching space than a cage.

Do not keep your cat in a basement or garage. Basements are dull, dark, and lead to boredom, uncleanliness and poor behavior. Garages are either too hot or too cold.

Wherever you confine your kitten, be sure to have a dish of water, a little dry food, a clean litterbox and a few safe toys. Our little Simon has a small cat bed, but it is not necessary. A rug or blanket will do.

Regardless of where you put the kitten's food dish, always feed in the same place. Even snacks should be carried to the dish while the kitten is still young. By establishing one feeding place, you will discourage your cat from walking the kitchen counter in search of food as he matures. When there are also dogs living in the same home, it will be necessary to find a kitchen shelf or desk to feed the cat upon. If not, you will have a fat dog and a skinny cat. I have never known a dog that wouldn't eat all available cat food.

Cats enjoy nibbling and should be allowed to work out their own feeding schedule unless it becomes too demanding. Skipping a meal once a week, once the cat has matured,

9

will help keep the cat's appetite sharp and prevent a fussy eater.

Until the kitten is four or five months old, working owners should arrange for someone to visit him at lunchtime. A little freedom to roam the house after eating, and of course some loving attention, will help him through those long, lonely days. Toys are important, too. They help develop a fun-loving disposition and insure strong muscular coordination through playful leaping, twisting, and turning.

Kittens need a great deal of sleep. Even when the family is home, allow the kit to sleep whenever he wishes. The waking hours will then be fun for both the kitten and the family.

Since everyone loves to hold a kitten, teach the children to sit on the floor to hold their pet. If you insist on this, you will never have him injured by jumping from someone's arms.

Now: Relax, keep your sense of humor, and enjoy the delightful antics and diversions your kitten will think up. No other animal is as innovative and playful as the graceful feline.

A SCHEDULE FOR BUSY FAMILIES

Busy families today must be well organized to insure that all household pets are well cared for AND taught to behave correctly when left alone. A schedule of the cat's daily food and activities taped to the refrigerator door is by far the most efficient method I have found. Your schedule should provide the following information, and any other comments you wish to add.

TIME	ACTIVITY	RESPONSIBILITY
Morning 7:00 to 8:00	Breakfast-½c cat food, check water dish. Put cat in his own room.	Child's, as he is the last to leave home.

TIME	ACTIVITY	RESPONSIBILITY
Noon 12:00 to 1:00	Feed kitten again, give some love and attention. Put cat back in own room.	Any family member who comes home for lunch.
After school 3:00 to 4:00	Allow kitten out of room. Play and take care of him until the family comes home.	Child
Evening dinner 5:00 to 6:00	Evening meal	Any family member

With family's busy evening activities, it's easy to forget to take care of the cat. Your child may need a reminder to check kitty's sleeping area. The litter box must be cleaned and fresh water and food provided. If possible, the cat and child should be allowed to sleep together.

Along with the cat's daily schedule, you will find it convenient to tape another sheet on the refrigerator with kitten's "Do's" and "Dont's."

DON'T ALLOW THE cat in Mom and Dad's bedroom. Please keep the door closed.

TAKE THE CAT outside with you when you have the time to stay with him. He cannot stay out alone.

DO NOT LET the cat scratch the furniture. Chase him away with a newspaper or give him a gentle shake.

BE SURE THE cat is locked in his room if you are the last person to leave the house.

BE CAREFUL THAT the cat doesn't slip out of the open door when you enter or leave.

FEED THE CAT if you come home and he seems hungry. No one is perfect and the responsible person has either forgotten or been delayed.

Once you have established the schedule and assigned the task, the parents must insist that the routine be followed. You'll be amazed at the responsibility your child will assume when he/she has the schedule to follow, and of course, a few gentle reminders from Mom or Dad.

TEACHING YOUR CAT TO BE A LOVING FAMILY MEMBER

Nearly all cats enjoy and crave attention and affection, if they are lovingly handled from birth. Lack of time to give each kitten enough handling while young is a common problem both breeders and eventual owners of kittens face today. We must realize, however, that each kitten differs in personality and intelligence, and each requires careful training to help him adjust to a new home and environment.

Often the same litter will produce a few kits so wild and peppy they climb the curtains and destroy the furniture, while their brothers and sisters are so shy they run and hide at the slightest noise. Whatever the temperament, each kit must be handled and taught to enjoy the companionship of his new owner. The wild kitten must learn to become tame and controlled and the shy one must be helped to overcome his fears.

Our two cats, Eleanor and Heathcliff, are good examples of differing intelligence and disposition. Eleanor, at three months of age, was one of those shy, quiet kittens, easy to have around, but not very receptive to training. The poor little kit also lacked personality and was rarely playful. Heathcliff, a half-grown stray, part Siamese, lived in our garage for a week before I could get near enough to touch him. Once in the house, he became wild and excitable—a whirlwind of mistrust and fury.

Fortunately, our family had enough experience and interest to help each cat overcome his individual problems.

THE SHY KITTEN

Eleanor was the easiest to train. As the two cats grew older, she also enjoyed her relationship with Heathcliff, as well as with the family. Fortunately Eleanor was a patient cat, as it was her destiny to always give way when Heathcliff, her impetuous playmate, demanded.

I began Eleanor's training by confining her to the smallest room in the house, so the elusive kitten could not escape under the furniture. I sat on the floor to prevent injury, should she jump from my arms.

Knowing that cats are frightened if held cradled on their backs like babies, I calmly picked up the kitten and positioned her rear hips and legs under my left elbow. Bringing my left hand forward under the cat's chest, I held her front legs comfortably separated by my fingers, so the kitten's body was secure and controlled. The right hand, still free, could be used for discipline, should the kitten bite, or for soothing, petting and calming her fears.

I scratched Eleanor's ears, talked quietly, and insisted she remain agreeable. Sometimes she would rebel and try to bite my finger. A quiet "no," together with a gentle tap on the nose, stopped her small resistance. As soon as she once again became docile, I praised the kitten and gave her some butter to lick from my finger. *I always reinforce my cats' good behavior with petting and praise.* An occasional treat of food is also very effective.

Since Eleanor was such a young kitten, she quickly learned to behave and even enjoyed being handled. The more affection our family showered on her, the more people-oriented, loving and demonstrative Eleanor became. The cat's behavior reinforced our feeling that all family pets need discipline as well as love, in order to become acceptable, well-adjusted members. In return, the family respected the kitten's occasional need for privacy and allowed her to view the world from her window seat, undisturbed for hours on end.

THE STRONG-WILLED CAT

Heathcliff, frightened and fearful from unknown past experiences, ate our food, but hissed and glowered at anyone who came too close. He had lived in our house for over a week, spending most of his time on the seat of a chair under the dining room table. Each time we extended a hand, we were met with slashing claws and a frightened retreat. Clearly we could not allow him to live in such fear.

When I began Heathcliff's training, I wore leather ski gloves which neither tooth nor claw could penetrate. Twice a day, morning and night, week after week, I held my frightened cat, using the same technique that I had found so successful when training Eleanor. But what a difference. Heathcliff, with all his feline fury, growled, writhed and threw his body in vain attempts to escape my grasp. When escape was impossible, Heathcliff literally tried to bite the hand that fed him.

It took many weeks to win Heathcliff's confidence and at first many sessions were a failure. It became evident that a few disciplinary taps, snaps and pinches were required to teach the cat to have a soft bite and velvet paws. Every few days some small progress would be evident as a little reward for my effort. Before long, Heathcliff would walk around the kitchen as he shared Eleanor's enthusiasm for snatching forbidden treats. Eventually, he learned to enjoy the family's attention and affection.

A year later, Heathcliff, along with Eleanor, now rubs against my legs to purr with love and satisfaction. Occasionally he will even jump into a family member's lap to spend a quiet hour or so. There are still a few indications of the stress Heathcliff suffered during the early months before we knew and loved him; but who knows, perhaps over the years, the past will blurr as the cat's future becomes more and more secure.

I am proud of Heathcliff's progress and hope that by sharing his story, others will be encouraged to give their cats discipline and training along with love and attention.

DEVELOPING YOUR CAT'S PERSONALITY

Standing at the kitchen sink, peeling potatoes in preparation for the evening meal, I suddenly became alert. That eerie feeling of someone watching was slowly interrupting my thoughts. "Oh no," I suddenly realized. "It's Charlie again." Whirling about to look for my cat in his favorite spot on top of the refrigerator, I barely had time to yell, "No!" before the soft bundle of fur hurled through space into my quickly outstretched arms.

"Very funny, Charlie," I said sarcastically, while hugging the spoiled beast.

"Good catch, Ma," he replied by rubbing his furry chin against mine.

This is one of Charlie's best and least endearing tricks. As a full-grown boy, he is now a heavy catch. If I had tried to teach him such an advanced trick, he would have rebelled. He thought up this performance on his own while a small kitten, and "Ma" didn't discourage him. She did, in fact, encourage him, so the habit has persisted into adulthood.

Charlie was a funny, loving, impetuous Siamese kitten who wallowed in the love and attention of a family of parents, children, dogs, fish and gerbils. Now, as an adult, he is far from the perfect cat, but has a personality all his own.

How do you raise a cat to be loving, sociable and have an interesting personality? It isn't difficult. With the proper upbringing, every cat can be personable—even today, when so many are necessarily left alone while their families are at work.

If your cats were raised in the wild, like their cousins, the pumas, cougars and lions, they would spend most of their lives dozing in the sun. In fact, they would sleep or doze, on and off, 15 to 20 hours out of every 24. This is one of the reasons domestic cats make such good pets for busy people. Household cats, as well as their wild relatives, don't mind being left alone for long periods of time. Once past their exuberant kittenish stage, most cats seem perfectly content to sleep the day away, as long as food, water and litter pan are readily available.

Anyone can raise a boring, uninteresting and uninterested cat by simply providing for their needs and otherwise ignoring them. *Cats like all living creatures need lots of attention to develop into fun-loving companions with personalities of their own.*

Cats raised exclusively indoors are usually more sociable than those who spend most of their time outside. A cat allowed outside spends comparatively little time in close contact with family members. When he does come inside, he's usually too tired for anything but sleep. Of course, given the choice, the cat will never be around when strangers call.

The indoor cat, on the other hand, will be well-rested, happy and mentally alert when the family comes home in the evening. Since his entire life is focused on the household activities, he will be eager for play and companionship.

Most cat owners enjoy interacting with their pets. As a child, I remember visiting the local "cat lady," a kind, somewhat eccentric old woman who lived for the pleasure and companionship of her 15 or so cats. She spent most of her day wearing a colorful housedress under an old, full-length bathrobe that flowed along as she walked. As she moved around her house, cats appeared from all directions to stalk, pounce upon, ambush and attack her trailing robe.

In imitation of my friend, as I grew older, I frequently entertained both cats and family by tying a sash to my waist and playfully dashed about the house with the cats in hot pursuit. As I became busier or less energetic (or perhaps smarter), I found it was much simpler to attach a sash to a doorknob, tie a knot at the other end, and allow my cats endless hours of fun and exercise. Eventually I learned to make this entertainment even more enjoyable by adding a few embellishments.

MAKING A DOORKNOB TOY

I did this by cutting a sash or cord into three unequal lengths, tying them together at one end and fastening them to the doorknob. I then took three pingpong balls and marked spots on two opposite sides of each one. Small holes were cut at each of the marked places. One piece of the hanging sash or cord was threaded through the holes of each ball. A very large knot was firmly tied at the end of the material, so that it could not possibly come loose. This setup allows your cats to chase the bouncing balls with no risk of losing them under the furniture.

Since cats are playful and imaginative by nature, it doesn't take expensive toys to entertain them. A small ball or piece of paper placed in the bathtub will amuse a cat for hours. An empty spool, cork or catnip mouse will stretch your feline hunter's imagination and provide the exercise needed for a firm, healthy body. An empty bag, box or newspaper on the floor is a delightful find for a curious cat.

Don't be surprised if your cat becomes very attached to a special toy. My son-in-law David laughed as he told me his story of FozzieBear and the mouse.

Last Christmas our daughter Carrie made and gave each cat in our family a catnip felt mouse. This gift soon became Fozzie's favorite toy. He took the mouse to his

bed, outside, and back in again. It soon became the most bedraggled of all his possessions. By this time, Linda was throwing the mouse outside each time she found it on the carpet. No sooner out, than Fozzie brought it in.

Finally David took the mouse to the garage and threw it into a garbage bag for disposal. Two days later, Fozzie brought it back into the house. Again David threw the mouse away in the bag. Again Fozzie dove to the bottom of the huge bag to retrieve his much prized toy.

No one knows how long David and Fozzie Bear would have kept up the game because Linda put an end to it by mending and patching Fozzie's mouse and there-after allowed the felt rodent to reside in the house with Fozzie and his family.

BUILD GOOD PLAYTIME BEHAVIOR

Most of the time, you can give your cat attention with barely a pause in your own activity. Talking to your pet, a most important stimulant for developing an imaginative and affectionate personality, can be done while fixing a meal, making a bed or writing a book. It's not what you say that counts, but the way you say it. I have read checkbooks, letters and invoices to my cats. These were received with the same great enthusiasm given my most spirited rendition of a favorite song. The important thing is a soft, enthusiastic tone; the affection you are communicating is much more basic than words.

As you can see, helping your cat to develop a pleasing personality is not difficult. You must remember, though, that along with the fun, your cat must learn acceptable behavior. Many times, behavior that is delightful in a kitten is totally unacceptable in an adult cat. For example, allowing your kitten to ambush and pounce upon your foot or ankle may be funny when the claws are small and teeth harmless, but you'll find yourself resenting those attacks as the cat gets older. Wagging fingers or wiggling toes for your kitten to attack is also encouraging behavior you won't appreciate when he is grown.

On the positive side, we all enjoy playing on a bed with our cats. Placing our hands under the blanket and tempting the cat to attack is good fun and can be permitted into adulthood. No one gets hurt, and the cat doesn't associate the attack with bare skin, since the blanket is always between tooth and hand.

Helping your cat to develop a happy, outgoing personality will bring its own reward. Your loving companion will continue to amuse, delight, surprise and fascinate you for many hours.

TOUCHING—A HAND AND PAW COMMUNICATION

As I pushed the key into the lock and hurriedly flung the back door open, I realized how late it had become. Rushing into the house, I dumped my packages on the dining room table and immediately went to the kitchen hoping to start dinner before the family arrived.

When I finally paused in front of the open cupboard door to make a selection, I felt the soft fur of our half-grown cat, Teddy, rub against my leg. Of course, the affectionate rub was accompanied by his usual conversation. Paying little attention to the kitten, I said the usual, "I'm glad to see you, too, Teddy," as I turned my back to continue my preparations.

I immediately forgot the cat as my mind flitted over a dozen more important concerns. With enough done in the kitchen, I walked into the living room and started up the stairs. As I passed the large, flat newel post at the bottom of the steps, I felt a swat on my arm. I had taken another two steps before I realized that what I had felt was not just a pat. Indeed, it was a rather hard smack!

Surprised, I paused to look, then stepped back to stand eye to eye with my usually good natured cat.

Teddy, pulling himself upright, full of dignity and indignation, started to bawl me out. The kitten was obviously distraught and trying to tell me something. I stood there absolutely dumbfounded.

After a few moments, the disgust and antagonism disappeared from the kitten's voice and it became lower and softer. He finally stopped talking and sat looking sad and alone. Teddy had been obviously upset and I had callously disregarded his small request. Feeling guilty, I put my face close to him to say how sorry I was and promised we would look into his problem. Soon we were nose touching nose, a position Teddy always favored when carrying on a conversation. We murmured a few more words to each other and then I felt his gentle forgiving paw softly caress my cheek.

Of all household pets, none enjoys touching more than the cat. Physical contact to him is absolutely necessary for sound mental and emotional health. Like other animals, felines have areas of the body which are more sensitive to touch than others.

Picture your cat as it curls up asleep on your lap. The underpart of the body is next to you, and the ears, neck, back and tail are exposed, inviting your touch. Cats enjoy head petting, ear scratching, back rubbing and tail stretching. The skin sensors in these areas produce mostly pleasurable sensations. Touch the pads of your pet's feet, though, and the immediate reaction is withdrawal. The "oh, so sensitive" foot pads are not to be touched.

The rough, thick skin covering the cat's feet contain the body's sweat glands and layers of fat which cushion the tough outer surface. Though the pads of his feet are tough, they are extremely sensitive to touch and temperature. Almost every object a cat encounters is touched, patted and finally batted by the paw, as kitty determines the desirability of the contact.

The hairless areas of the cat's body also includes the nose, which is padded up to 75 times thicker than other parts of the body. Each cat's nose is ridged in a pattern so individual that a feline nose print is as distinctive as the

24

human fingerprint. His nose has pigment for color, nerve fibers and very sensitive sensory receptors, which respond to pressure and temperature.

You usually get a mixed reaction when rubbing your pet's stomach. At times he will relax, roll about and enjoy. Other times the claws flash out and you are reminded to keep your hands off this often touchy area. The stomach is one of the most vulnerable parts of a cat's body. It is also sensitive to touch. It takes a cat that lives in harmony with himself to allow his stomach to be rubbed. With gentle stroking, the cat's muscles relax, and the heart rate decreases, allowing the body systems to slow down.

BONDING BUILDS LOVE

Touching, if it is started while the cat is young, binds you and your pet for life. In fact, many times an orphan cat will not thrive because he lacks physical contact with his mother. Since cats are socially dependent animals, deprivation of affection is damaging to a kitten's emotional and physical development.

The best example of bonding is between mother and offspring. When a parent cat licks and grooms its offspring, the digestive tract is activated and circulation improves, producing healthy alert youngsters.

The hair over most of a cat's body is lubricated with oily secretions from the sebaceous glands. These help to waterproof the coat and give it a healthy shine. The sebaceous glands also secrete cholesterol, which is converted to vitamin D by sunlight. As the cat grooms, it ingests this valuable nutrient.

Fear of being touched is often the result of poor handling during kittenhood, or lack of human contact during the early formative weeks of life. This early contact between animal and human is a strong and necessary bond.

When you hold and stroke your pet, a general feeling of well-being is shared. Bonding builds a trusting, secure relationship between individuals. In some cases, such as when a stray cat "adopts" a new owner, bonding is instigated by the cat. Bonding can also occur between two cats or between a dog and a cat.

All cat lovers know that as each kitten grows, he develops an individual personality and assumes his own quirks of behavior. This is what makes each of our cats so endearing to us. We should remember, however, that no matter how dissimilar our cats are in looks, behavior and attitude, it is a fact that there are certain patterns to which all cats conform.

Touching is the most noticeable and certainly the most enjoyable form of cat communication. It can also transmit other emotions: anger, jealousy and fear, for instance. This was demonstrated by my cat, Teddy, when he finally lost all patience with me and gave me a sharp swat to gain the attention he needed.

When I put my face against Teddy's soft forehead, my touch communicated an inner feeling to him. I said, "I'm sorry. All will be well soon."

As Teddy's paw caressed my cheek, I received his inner communication. "I forgive you and everything is fine again."

TEACHING "COME" WHEN CALLED

Bonding will instill in your kitten the desire to be with you. Since all love and care is provided by his family, naturally all fun and satisfaction comes when the cat is near the people he loves. There is no need to teach your kitten to "come" when called if he has developed a strong individual identification through your loving bond. In fact, at least half of the time, you may not be able to get him out from underfoot.

You are defeating yourself when you call "here kitty, kitty." Your cat may answer, but usually only if he is hungry or wishes to come in the house.

Teach your cat his name and use it repeatedly. While holding, petting and playing, talk to him saying his name frequently. Within a short time, you'll be amazed to find that your cat will come each time you call him correctly.

You never hear dog owners call their dog with "here

doggie, doggie.'' The reason they use their dog's name is because the pet associates better with his own identification.

Cats respond to their own identifying name in the same way. Being taught and called by his individual name builds a sense of pride and a bonding relationship within the family.

SCRATCHING—A NECESSARY RITUAL

Daily scratching is a self-grooming ritual for cats. It is as necessary and normal to a feline as eating and sleeping. Scratching is not only a vital activity in a cat's life, it is also enjoyable. Each time your cat carries out this instinctive ritual, he enjoys a good stretch and at the same time gives himself a pedicure.

The old lore that cats sharpen their claws by scratching is only partially true. We now know that the claws of domestic cats are covered by a sheath. This thin tissue, much like our own fingernails, continually grows. As the cat scratches, this outer sheath falls away leaving a new sharp claw.

When our cats scratch in the litter box, on the floor around the food dish, or on the scratching post, we take little notice. Not so when we see them dig their claws into the upholstery of a favorite chair or the living room drapes! Our tempers flare as we imagine dollar bills floating by in a flurry of shredded fabric. Certainly this rambunctious feline must be taught where he may and may not scratch. What's more, the lesson must begin immediately.

Since cats, especially indoor cats, are going to scratch somewhere, the first step toward a well-behaved animal is to provide acceptable toys and scratching places. Why toys? Because if you give them adequate areas for exercise and diversified entertainment, it is unlikely that your pets will become obsessed with any one activity, such as excessive scratching or soiling. Destructive behavior is often the result of boredom and loneliness

As for providing acceptable scratching places, there are many kinds of scratching posts—from the simple homemade pad to the elaborate floor-to-ceiling cat trees that are commercially available. Whichever type you choose, you may find that you have to teach your cat to use it. Rub a little catnip into the material to get his interest and rub his paws up and down on the surface several times to show him what you expect.

MATERIAL FOR SCRATCHING POST

Most felines enjoy carpeting, burlap or denim materials—if a good tree trunk isn't available. You can make your own scratching post by nailing one of these materials onto a sturdy post—perhaps even a stairway post—or a flat surface. I lightly pad a 36-inch square board, cover it with my pet's favorite fabric and nail it to a door or wall near the cat's sleeping area. *Cats love to stretch and scratch after a nap*.

Remember, too, that cats will naturally be attracted to furniture covered in burlap and denim fabrics. When buying, avoid open weaves and rough textures. As a further deterrent, place your furniture so it doesn't become part of his pathway. Watch him to see where he likes to sit or nap. If he finds it convenient to climb up the leather sofa to get to the window ledge, you are asking for trouble. You can make life easier for both yourself and your cat if you provide a cat perch with a small ladder—and move the sofa.

Moving the sofa may be an easy solution to the climbing problem, but what if your cat has decided to use that same sofa arm for his daily scratching? In this case you have two alternatives: either learn to live with shredded furniture (which many cat owners do), or insist that your pet stop the destruction immediately and permanently. *It's really not hard if you remember that you are smarter than your cat and you set the rules.*

GENTLE EARLY TRAINING

Let's start with training the younger cat since this will avoid more severe discipline in later years. Decide beforehand which areas will be off-limits for your pet. Of course, he will pick his favorite spots, and he should be allowed to do so whenever possible, but you have the power to veto his decisions and the ability to make off-limit places so uncomfortable that your cat will "decide" that he doesn't really like them after all.

From three months on, kittens become a whirlwind of activity. They are fiesty, hard to catch, and will disappear at the first sign of disagreement. It is, therefore, necessary to confine the kitten when you cannot or do not wish to supervise his activities. Allow your pet out of this restricted area only when you have the time to train and play with him.

When you are ready, release the kitten and give him some much-needed attention. Being a normal cat, he will

30

probably be full of energy after spending most of his day napping. Before long, he will approach the forbidden furniture. When he does, walk quickly to the kitten, pick him up, give him a little shake, say "no" firmly, and take your kitten to the scratching post. Show him the proper place to scratch by gently rubbing his paws up and down on the post while speaking soothingly.

If you start teaching your kitten while he is young and follow through by punishing each forbidden act, your reward will be a loving, nondestructive adult cat. But if he missed this kind of kitten training, the gentle discipline described here will probably not work now. If he has been scratching the furniture and getting away with it for months, or even years, stronger measures are in order.

NAIL CLIPPING

As a first deterrent to household destruction, I always keep my cat's claws clipped and filed to prevent snagging. Clipping is not difficult if you plan ahead. Choose a time when your cat has just eaten and is taking one of his frequent naps. If you work fast, you can usually clip the nails before your pet is fully awake and ready to resist. I use a guillotine-type clipper that allows me to insert the nail tip through a hole and snip off only the end.

Of course, early training makes this task easier. If you clip kitty's claws from the time you bring him into your home, the task will soon become routine. When necessary, wrap your little friend in a towel or large net bag, confining all but the paw you are working on. This will allow you to continue without risking bodily injury.

PART 2

The Nobody's Home Cat Grows Up

KITCHEN MANNERS FOR OUR CAT

Many cat owners are convinced their pets cannot be trained. In fact, they believe their cats have the right to indulge themselves, behaving as they please.

I find no objection to this thinking as long as an owner has the time and patience to cater to his or her cat's every whim. I have found, however, during 20 years of raising, living with and loving cats, that too much indulgence and too little expectation on the owner's part lead to poor behavior from the cats and eventual unhappiness for the patient, but exhausted, owner.

While it is certainly true that cats are nonconformists by nature, they can be easily trained—if you teach a lesson your cat wishes to learn.

As I sit watching Fancy, our new kitten, dart across the kitchen floor in pursuit of a small ball of cellophane, I remember a lesson taught to our first Siamese kitten many years ago.

While working in the kitchen one evening, I tripped over Charlie, our talkative, cross-eyed Siamese. As he demanded equal rights to an immediate dinner, his companion cat, Thomasina, a quiet calico, flitted about the floor searching for crumbs. Busily carrying a pot of hot soup from stove to table, the thought struck me that I could have easily tripped over either pet and hurt both the cats and myself. I resolved henceforth to lock the cats out of the kitchen during meal time.

While I paused, thinking over my problem, I happened to glance at our two family dogs, each sitting on her allotted rug, patiently watching the now familiar evening scene. I had taught the dogs ''go to your rugs'' and ''stay'' to keep them out from underfoot while I worked in the kitchen. Why not, I reasoned, teach the cats acceptable kitchen manners?

Teaching them was so easy that over the years, I have taught the same trick to every cat our family has owned. I think both you and your cat will be delighted if he learns this "good cat" trick called, "go to your place."

When a kitten is four to six months old, he is able to jump up on chairs, tables and countertops. In fact, cats much prefer to view the world while looking down.

Realizing this, I knew our cats would never accept sitting on a floor rug like the dogs. I chose, instead, a pair of wooden stools. When not in use, they were pushed side by side under the kitchen table. Any desk or shelf will work as well, as long as the cats are close enough to feel that they can get your attention.

For the first lesson, which was held before dinner when the cats were hungry, I pulled the stools out and slightly away from the table. I then patted the hard, wood surface to make a drumming sound as I called the cats.

Of course, the reluctant felines sat a few feet away ignoring me. I immediately walked over, squatted down and dangled a piece of meat by each of their noses, patting the stools again as I lured the cats to jump up on the chosen seats. For the first two lessons, each cat went as far as the stools, but balked at jumping on the seats. No fuss! I just refused to give them the treat and stopped the lesson.

The third day both cats jumped up on their stools and, once properly seated, were instantly rewarded with the enticing tidbits they were eagerly trying to snatch from my hands. Along with their rewards, the pets were also given lavish praise for their outstanding performances.

From that day until our cats learned to jump up on the stools whenever I patted them, we served all food, including meals, on the stools. Each time food was given, the stools were patted to teach the cats to associate the sound with food and where they must go to get it.

During the training period, every time the cats took their places on their stools, they were rewarded with a small treat. It didn't take our glutton, Charlie, long to figure out the whole show. He became devoted to sitting on his stool and carrying on conversations with anyone who walked by. Thomasina, always the lady, sat and looked primly sweet, only occasionally murmuring a request for her share of attention.

If at any time during the training period the cats chose to be disagreeable, and continued to sit at my feet meowing, they were ignored. Between the tidbits and their regular meals, it didn't take the pets long to run into the kitchen at the first sound of meal preparations. They would immediately jump up on their stools, and being safely out from underfoot, wait patiently for their expected treat.

CLASSY CAT TRICKS

"Mom, come quick!" Lisa yelled as I hurried into the kitchen. I was surprised to see her flat on her stomach watching her kitten, Thomasina, daintily dip her paw into a glass of milk, gracefully hold the paw above her nose and, with superb cat manners, lick the milk off her paw.

Lisa, now grown and married, called a few days ago to tell us about the abandoned, half-grown kitten her husband Phil had found and brought home from work. "You'll never guess what I just taught him," laughed Lisa.

"Bet I can," I replied. "Hasn't everyone in our family taught each kitten the same 'paw in the glass' trick?"

It's fun to teach tricks to your cat, and many enjoy the attention they receive when performing. Most cats are natural actors already, and some are real hams, so it's not hard to teach them tricks if you use the right approach.

I always enjoyed watching our two cats, Thomasina and Charlie, come into the kitchen, jump up on stools that sat side by side and wait patiently for their snacks.

After I taught the cats to sit on their own stools, I taught them to "speak." Teaching Charlie to talk was easy since he was an outgoing, totally charming Siamese. Thomasina had an entirely different personality; she was quiet, calm and inclined to allow Charlie to speak for them both.

Teaching Thomasina to meow was the hardest part of the routine. I had to hold Thom's front paws on the stool and tantalize her to speak by dangling a piece of meat in front of her nose. She wanted to sit up and bat at the food, but I refused to allow her to do so. Finally, in desperation, she would meow. I immediately gave her the food and lots

39

of praise. Of course, I always used the key word, "speak," for this trick.

"Sit up" was the last part of the series of tricks I wanted the cats to perform while they sat on their stools. This was easy. I held a tasty tidbit over their heads, and the cats quickly learned to sit up while trying to snatch the food. I never allowed them to get the morsel by grabbing it, then disappearing. This would have defeated the purpose, as they would have refused to perform, if they could have snatched and run. Our friends were very impressed (especially the so-called cat haters) when the cats ran into the kitchen, jumped up on their stools, sat up and meowed for their treats.

After I taught our pets to jump up on their stools when I patted the seat, I found that they agreed to jump up on any surface I tapped. This was an added pleasure for family members who needed only to pat the cushion they were sitting on to have one or both cats join them immediately. Naturally, they received lots of affection to reward their performances.

The best time to teach a cat most tricks is when he is hungry, but "roll over" is best taught when he is just waking up from a good rest. Kitty will be both relaxed and a little hungry as he stretches out on the floor. Kneeling beside him, dangle food enticingly near his nose and encourage him to roll from one side to the other as you make a half circle with the food. You may have to use your other hand to push him from one side to the other. It won't take kitty long to realize that rolling about takes little time and effort and the rewards are great.

With repeated training, your pet will follow your hand with or without food in it. Each time he performs, repeat the command, "roll over," so the words become part of his vocabulary.

Another accepted method of teaching the "roll over" trick is with a gentle tickle on the reclining cat's stomach. If he isn't too ticklish, he will usually roll over. Many of my cats have playfully attacked my hand instead of rolling over, so I prefer using food as a stimulant to encourage them to perform. Perhaps a combination of the two may work well for you and your pet.

I enjoy teaching our cats to jump over a stick. This trick is easy to teach and fun to watch. It is best taught when your pet is in a playful mood and hungry enough to follow food used as a lure. Use a rod or stick that is rigid, but lightweight and comfortable to hold. Starting at floor level, lure the cat back and forth across the stick with a treat. After a little practice to assure him that the stick is harmless, raise it off the floor slightly. Gradually increase the height of the stick in subsequent sessions. As long as the cat can walk over the stick, you'll have no problems.

When the stick gets high enough that he must jump over to get the treat, you will have to proceed slowly, and at times go back to a lower level. If he is familiar with walking on a leash, this is a perfect time to encourage kitty, with gentle tugs, to jump over the hurdle.

Be patient. Work at each height for awhile and do not push him to go too high too soon. I prefer to teach this trick in a narrow hallway so he cannot conveniently walk around the stick to obtain the treat.

Finally, to borrow a phrase, you **can** teach an old cat new tricks—at least some of the less strenuous ones. You'll be surprised how much both you and your cat will enjoy the compliments.

JEALOUSY OVER NEW BABY

A new baby in the home threatens a cat which has monopolized all of his owner's love and attention. The ugly horns of jealousy rise and the senior pet retaliates. What better way to pay you back than misbehave under the guise of innocence.

Household pets are masters of retaliation. Many times their jealousy is demonstrated by scratching on forbidden furniture, nipping, refusing to eat, or ignoring previously obeyed commands.

When you bring a baby into your home, advanced preparations are necessary to help your cat accept the new family member. Let's look at this situation from your cat's point of view.

For several months your pet cat sensed an air of excitement and expectation in the house. He has been annoyed by the occasional changes in routine, but enjoyed playing with the interesting packages wrapped in gay, crinkly paper. Exploring the newly decorated nursery and playing on the ladder left during decorating was great entertainment. All told, life has been stimulating and fascinating for this fun-loving feline.

Suddenly the household changes. The excitement is gone, the rooms empty and quiet. Though the food dish is full, life has become dull and lonely because his best friend has disappeared—but not for long.

Soon the cat's loved ones come home bringing a new family member wrapped in a soft, warm blanket. The cat

42

is naturally curious and eagerly jumps upon the bed where the infant is laying.

Your reaction during this introduction is important to the future happiness of your whole family. Allow the cat to smell the baby he is going to watch grow up.

Over the next few months, the cat will react to baby in his own way. With every new sound, at each feeding and bath, he will be around to investigate. He may become devoted to this new and interesting toy, or perhaps find the whole routine boring and merely observe from a distance. If the cat shows signs of jealousy, you can easily give him extra attention when baby sleeps.

Every owner knows that cats love to be warm. They will take naps on top of furnaces and registers, snuggle up to hot lamp shades, and nap in the clothes dryer if given a chance.

When a cat is looking for a warm, comfortable place to sleep, what could be more soft and inviting than sharing a bed with baby? The bed is in an area where a cat can catch a few winks in peace and baby is warm and cuddly to lie against.

I have raised babies and cats together for many years and I'm sure that cats will not deliberately harm an infant, but since newborn babies are so helpless it's better to be safe and keep felines and babies apart when you cannot supervise their activities.

HELPFUL SAFETY SUGGESTIONS

If your new baby sleeps in a small bassinet, it is especially important to keep your cat out of the room. If a large feline jumps and hangs on the side of a lightweight bassinet, baby, bed and cat may come tumbling. Even when using a full size crib you'll need to keep your cat out of the sleeping area for a few months.

Since most parents are uncomfortable with the door to the nursery closed, remove the wood door and replace it with a screen door. This will keep your pet out, but allow you to hear every sound coming from the room.

Allow your cat to share in family activities. When you feed the baby, offer your pet dinner or a treat at the same time. You will also find that many of your happiest hours will be spent playing on the bed or floor with baby and the cat.

As your child grows, teach him or her to protect and be gentle with animals. A child must learn to control all affectionate exuberance, for the cat's sake. Just as your cat will not harm the baby deliberately, your child does not mean to harm the family's much loved pets. *Both child and cat must be carefully guarded and trained during their early years while learning to live together.*

REPELLING THE ATTACK

Almost all cat owners will agree that an attacking cat is merely behaving in an instinctive way. That is, though the cat lives in harmony with humans, he still retains the inherited hunting traits—stalking and attacking—of his wild ancestors.

It's also reasonable to assume that an attacking cat has either been allowed to develop an undesirable attacking habit, or is living in such a stressful situation that he has reverted to fighting back as a defense. There is a reason when a normal, loving cat becomes aggressive. If you can find and eliminate that reason, he can be retrained much easier.

Begin by ruling out disease, infection or other physical disorders. Have your cat thoroughly checked by a veterinarian. If he is physically healthy, you should search for emotional disturbances.

Rough handling, loud noises and family fighting are just a few causes of severe stress and emotional trauma for a cat. Some felines react to these situations by becoming listless, withdrawn and depressed. Others may become unmanageable, wild and hysterical.

Poor behavior may also occur when a cat has been mistreated, refused affection or handled violently during his growing years. In extreme cases, even love, understanding and patient care will not erase the deep inner hurt, or completely relieve the anxiety such a cat must live with constantly.

In many cases, undesirable attacking behavior is simply a case of improper training. Every cat owner knows the amusement of watching an impish kitten, body crouched, ears flattened and tail low, stealthily pursuing its prey. And we've all smiled as he wiggles his hips, swishes his tail and leaps to the attack. What fun for the kitten as the owner flashes a hand to tempt this behavior. Before the owner has time to notice, though, the kitten has modified the rules and perfected his strategy. He now attacks unsuspecting feet, as well. It doesn't matter—those little claws and baby teeth cause no pain.

But too soon he grows up. An adult cat who plays the

game of ambush and attack is no longer amusing. He attacks his owners and many times the owner's guests. How sad that he was allowed to grow up thinking this was acceptable behavior.

The cat is now confused and cannot understand why he is being punished for something that he was once encouraged to do. Fortunately, with patience and diligence, an owner can correct this behavior.

While the cat's harmful playing must be stopped, kicking and hitting him with a paper or your hand is not the way to retrain. This abuse could even make the situation worse by forcing the pet to retaliate.

Now is the time to use creative strategy since the cat thinks the attacking behavior is a fun game. When he is in an attacking mood, draw a peacock feather, scarf, or ball tied to a cord across the floor. Sometimes this simple distraction works quite effectively, especially with a younger cat. Still, it may take awhile until he prefers the distraction to your feet or hands, so be patient.

STRATEGY STOPS STALK AND STRIKE GAME

If a simple distraction doesn't work, try a combination of tempting the cat with a toy along with firm discipline to repel the attack. What else can be done to convince all but the most die-hard attacker that hands and feet are no longer fun to play with?

In addition to your distraction toy, arm yourself with a plastic spray bottle (available at any hardware or grocery store). Fill it with water, and if necessary, you may add a teaspoonful of cider vinegar to the water to make it more distasteful to the cat. Now, keeping the bottle in your hand but hidden from the cat's view, walk by and tempt him once again with your scarf or ball.

If the cat attacks the toy, great. This is exactly what you want. Play for a short time and praise your good pet. If, however, he attacks your feet as you walk by, say a firm "no" and immediately use the water spray. Kitty will react as all cats do by sulking, refusing food and maybe slashing out at you. Be kind to him otherwise, but continue your discipline each time he attacks the wrong object—you. Most cats find that stalking and attacking hands and feet are no longer fun after a few days of consistent discipline. If he resumes these attacks at some time in the future, you must immediately stop the game, or you'll be right back where you started.

If you can't stop the cat's attack before he latches onto your tender skin, or if he is a die-hard assailant who stalks and strikes with deadly earnest, sterner measures are in order. You may have to buy or borrow heavy gloves. With your hands protected, you will be able to grab the determined aggressor by the scruff of the neck and snap his nose with your thumb and forefinger to get him to release his grip. Then, hold him away from you, give him a good shake and a firm "no."

Once you have decided with firm determination that your cat must be brought under control, you may have to wear gloves each time you pet or pick him up. He will probably not like this situation, but if you remain calm, speak quietly, bribe him with favorite tidbits from your hand, and refuse to allow your ferocious feline to gain control again, you can win the battle.

In the end, if you impress upon your pet that he cannot always get his own way, you'll find the cat will calm down and both of you will start enjoying life together.

47

WALKING ON A LEASH

As a young bride, I brought my longhaired Persian, Muffie, to live with Jim and me in a city perched on the shores of beautiful Lake Michigan. Being a country cat, Muffie adjusted to the beach and rolling sand hills immediately and seemed to feel at home wherever her loved ones chose to live.

Muffie and I were constant companions, walking the beach, chasing crabs in the shallow pools and gazing into the water for hours on end. I think we would both have enjoyed living our lives out together in this most perfect spot. But like the wilting of a perfect flower, our serenity vanished as the cool fall days turned into winter's harsh disillusionment.

Since our cottage was only a summer residence, Jim and I decided to move into an apartment in the city. Muffie, of course, would come along. We thought she would become a city cat just as easily as she had accustomed herself to life by the water.

A few hours after we moved into our small apartment, Muffie and I had our first real disagreement. Being an outside cat, the stubborn feline refused to use her new litter box and insisted at the top of her lungs, that she be allowed to roam out of doors as she had always done.

I was shocked! This bossy loudmouth was a different cat than I had ever known. On top of that, the landlady who had reluctantly allowed us to house our cat, complained bitterly about every sound. Believing there was no other recourse, I put the cat outside and prayed she would find friends among the neighborhood cats and dogs. Most of all, I worried about the traffic on the busy streets surrounding us.

It didn't work. The dogs in the neighborhood clustered in groups as they roamed, belligerently terrifying every cat they could find. To make matters worse, since we lived on

the second floor and our windows were inaccessible, Muffie took to sitting on the outside ledge of the landlady's kitchen window. Muffie yowled, the landlady screamed, and I was in a panic.

What should I do? What could I do? To give my beloved cat away was totally unacceptable.

I finally decided that even though the cat had never worn a collar, and was three years old, she would have to learn to walk on a leash. I could then protect her from the dogs and she and I would once again enjoy the long companionable walks we both relished so much.

I began Muffie's training by placing a lightweight piece of cord around her neck to help her accept the collar that was to come. Although she occasionally caught her claws in the cord while scratching her neck, she seemed indifferent to the small hindrance.

Withing a few days, I removed the twine from Muffie's neck and replaced it with a narrow leather collar. The next step was to get the cat accustomed to moving with the pull of the collar.

First, I tied a short cord to Muff's collar and allowed her to drag it about the rooms until she got used to the feel of the new leash. Hooray! This was easily accomplished and the lessons proceeded.

Till now, I had not used food to help Muffie learn her lessons, but NOW was the time. The next step was to teach her to accept a person at the other end of the leash. I began by placing some butter on my finger and sitting on the floor. Then I tugged on my cat's leash, urging her to come to me. She resisted and I insisted. When she finally was pulled to my side, the tempting treat was offered.

After a week of outright bribery, I continued giving Muff her treat, along with extravagant praise for her good work. The next few days, I tapered off the food and increased my insistence that she walk where I wanted. Twice daily after our jaunts around the apartment, I gave the obedient cat her favorite morsel along with lavish praise.

Since Muffie refused to use her litter box, I had been taking her out doors three or four times a day. She had a favorite patch of dirt which she quickly used, then she was whisked back inside.

Two weeks of fairly successful indoor training finally

gave me the courage to take Muffie outside to play. Oh glorious day! I had tied a long cord on the cat's collar and we sat on the sweet smelling grass, watching autumn's final show of color as the last golden leaves fluttered down from the trees.

Muffie, flitting about chasing leaves and spying bugs, was unconcerned when she reached the end of the rope. I sat with my back against a tree, relaxed and occasionally murmured approval when my companion made an exceptional catch. Life was good that day.

Although Muffie was doing well, both in the apartment and in the yard, it became increasingly apparent that however her collar was put on, the cat could slip out of it, if she wanted. Obviously, the only answer was a strong lightweight harness which would be more comfortable and equalize the pressure from the pull of the leash.

That night I wound a cord around Muffie's chest behind the front legs, to her back and tied a knot. I then brought the cord up to her neck between the shoulders, to the collar and tied it securely. It was a secure, lightweight and comfortable harness.

The cat didn't react to the change, so I tied a leash to the makeshift harness and walked her around the apartment, once again encouraging her with soothing words of satisfaction.

Within a short time, Muffie was wearing a ready-made cat harness. It was a handsome ensemble. Even the landlady grudgingly admitted that my lovely grey cat looked stylish while wearing her red-jeweled leather harness with matching leash.

Oh yes, Muffie and I had a few ups and downs, and more than one disagreement over who was leading whom; but while each of us won or lost a few, we eventually learned to become a team.

The lessons were well worth the effort. Once again my beautiful Muff and I roamed the streets and parks, talking to each other, and discovering together that a city can also be a fascinating place to explore.

RIDING IN THE CAR

For many years our family has taught all our pets to ride in the car and enjoy every moment. It all started when we purchased our first Siamese cat many years ago. He was a handsome, cross-eyed, outspoken fellow who lived for six months as a country cat. Charlie was his name, and for the rest of his life, he adamantly refused to respond to any other.

Charlie loved riding in automobiles. He would sneak into any four-wheeled vehicle that moved—milk and bread trucks, repair vans and neighbor's cars. Since our family took frequent trips to a cottage at the lake, Charlie settled easily into the family routine.

Thomasina, a shy, quiet calico cat, joined our family a few years later. She and Charlie shared similar likes and dislikes, except Charlie's love for riding. Motor vehicles terrified Thomasina. Since we knew we would have to include Thom on the family visits to the lake, we opted to try teaching the reluctant feline to tolerate car rides.

I have since taught all our family cats, as well as friend's and neighbor's household pets to ride in a car and even to enjoy occasional trips. Here is how I did it.

Thomasina, being a quiet feline, was not as receptive to training as Charlie had been. I have found over the years that cats like Thomasina are often indifferent to all training and must have gentle, but firm discipline, while still young. I began Thom's training by sitting on the floor and holding her a few minutes at a time. I scratched her ear and talked soothingly, but insisted that she remain agreeable. If she began to fight back, I would slap her paws lightly or shake her gently to teach her to control her temper. As soon as she stopped her bad behavior, I immediately resumed the petting to reinforce her good attitude.

Since she was just a young kitten, she quickly learned to behave when she was handled. In return, the family respected her occasional need for privacy, and the cat training—for all of us, including Thomasina—progressed agreeably.

Teaching Thom to enjoy the family automobile was the next step. For training sessions, we tried to choose a time when the cat was in a quiet, contented mood. We picked her up, cuddled her, and quickly carried her out to the car. We sat quietly inside with the door open.

During the first week of training, Thom would almost immediately jump from our arms and leave the car; however, she did seem to enjoy walking over the soft seat to make her exit. She did not appear to be frightened, just alert in a strange area. We continued her training—a few minutes at a time—until she accepted staying in the car with no fear. Before long, Thom could not resist the spacious front seat and would sometimes leave our laps and sprawl across the seat cushion.

Amazing happenings occur when you teach your cat proper behavior. Thomasina became more people-oriented, loving and demonstrative. Our family, especially the children, learned that all family pets need discipline as well as love. We also discovered that since training was done only a few minutes at a time, it did not disrupt our daily schedule as much as we had feared. Every family member participated in the training and we enjoyed discussing Thomasina's progress.

Once she accepted the car and relaxed while walking about in the enclosure, we began to introduce the mechanical noises from the motor and the occasional buzzing seat belt that cats often find so frightening. We had once thoughtlessly allowed a cat to become terrified by the noise of the seat belt, and she never forgot the experience, although she did eventually become a quiet but reluctant car passenger.

As it turned out, the motor was not a problem. Thomasina seemed to ignore the soft, idling sound. Accelerator and brake noises were also accepted with relative ease.

FOOD AS TRAINING AID

Up to this time, we had not used food to help Thom adjust to the car. Now was the time to introduce enticing tidbits. At the next sitting, I was prepared with a small jar of pureed meat. Placing some meat on my finger, I offered Thomasina the treat as I released the seat belt and allowed it to buzz for only a second. Thom jumped at the sound, but greedily resumed licking her treat. I repeated the noise at short intervals, three times the first day and for several days thereafter. Before long, she could tolerate the buzz, even without food as a reinforcement.

I used baby food meat as an aid in Thomasina's training for two reasons. It was a great treat to her; and all my earlier cats had enjoyed licking meat or butter from my finger. Most of the time they continued to lick long after the treat was gone. From feline mother, to brothers and sisters, to pseudo-human parents, cats enjoy and learn by licking. Thomasina, as she licked and smelled my finger, began to identify this smell with security, love and discipline.

Animals have an intense desire to see where they are going. With Thomasina, it was easy to allow her to ride on the back of the front passenger seat since soft fabric upholstery was used in those days. With today's automobile, vinyl is a popular seat covering and it can easily become ruined by cat claws. While Thom and Charlie frequently rode on the seat back, or on a rug across the rear window, we have since found it more convenient, and much safer, if a car seat or cat perch is provided.

AN INNOVATIVE CAR SEAT

Had I known with Thom and Charlie what I figured out a little later with another cat, I would have trained all my cats from the very beginning to sit in a car seat. In fact, a few years ago, I found an old bicycle basket in the garage. We cleaned and repaired it, and a clever neighbor fitted the basket with hooks taken from a baby car bed. The basket was then hung facing forward over the passenger seat back. It became an ideal, attractive and safe cat car seat.

Several years and a few cats after that experience, I learned the ultimate secret in training a cat to enjoy using a car seat. Long before I began any training, I taught them to sleep in one as a bed inside the house. This became their favorite sleeping place, and when the bed was moved into the car, the training was the easiest I had ever done.

Once the cat was accustomed to the car noises as well as

the seat or perch, we drove the car up and down the driveway. This training will be much easier if you have someone to act as chauffeur.

With Thomasina, each trip was lengthened until all the noises became common sounds. Finally, the day came when Thom was content to share her companion Charlie's greatest joy—riding with the family in a moving four-wheel vehicle.

DISCIPLINE FOR OLDER CATS

Older cats will not respond to the gentle training used with kittens. This is especially true if your pet has been scratching the furniture and getting away with it. You have been defeating yourself if you have allowed your cat access to forbidden scratching areas while you were away from home, then scolded or hit him for the same behavior when you returned.

These conflicting signals cause the cat to become confused, sneaky and withdrawn. It's better to have the battle in the open and get it over with. Then, both you and your pet can retreat, lick your wounds, and begin to rebuild your relationship—this time based on mutual respect, as well as affection. As a mature cat owner, you should be able to take a few huffy snubs from your feline pet and realize that they won't last forever.

If you have already fallen into the trap of disciplining him only some of the time, don't despair. There is still

hope, but you will have to make up your mind—with absolutely no exceptions—that this naughtiness must stop.

You will have to isolate your cat in a cage or room, away from furniture he can scratch, when you are not able to supervise his activities. If you do this consistently, it won't be long before you will once again be able to give your pet freedom in the house at all times. What's more, after a day of work or play, you will be able to return home without shuddering at the thought of the damage he may have done while you were away.

EFFECTIVE EVENING TRAINING

After-dinner training sessions will be more effective if you establish a routine for the evening hours. It's probably already your practice to come home after work, let your pet loose and feed and play with him.

Don't forget how important it is to talk to your cat. Felines love verbal communication and will respond to familiar words. Talking is also the easiest way to give a pet attention when your hands are busy doing something else.

Later in the evening, take your cat into the area where the forbidden scratching has occurred. Make yourself comfortable and ignore him while you read or watch television. But stay alert and observe his movements out of the corner of your eye. When he starts to scratch, stop this misbehavior by using one of the following methods.

Spray the cat with water. A forceful stream of water from a spray bottle is one of the most common and successful methods of discipline used by cat owners. When the cat misbehaves and is caught in the act, give him a good squirt and accompany it with the verbal command "no." If your cat is one of the few who does not seem to mind being sprayed with plain water, add a small amount of cider vinegar as a little extra incentive. The vinegar will sting enough to make him uncomfortable, but will do no lasting damage. *As soon as the cat stops scratching, praise his good behavior.*

Spray the cat with air. This is an effective, but less severe (and less messy), means of discipline. The water spray works well if you are spraying it on material that will not be damaged; but the air spray has an obvious advantage if your cat is scratching a delicate fabric that will stain. You can purchase canisters of air at any photographic store. Some of the air cans have adjustable spray nozzles. Others have more, or less, air pressure depending on the brand. There is one air spray made of soft plastic that is squeezed like a bulb. This releases only a slight amount of air per squeeze.

I discovered this gentle method of discipline when I purchased a can of air to use when cleaning my camera. While using the air, I accidently sprayed one of my cats. His reaction was astounding. He hissed and jumped into the air, then sat back down and acted as if nothing happened. Since the cat didn't associate the source of irritation with me, he didn't even move away!

A week later, I used the same air spray on the same cat to discourage him from jumping onto the table. I hid under the table to make the discipline a complete surprise. After only three attempts, he decided to sit on the chair instead. I tend to believe that he associated the air spray with a hiss.

Remember, as with the water spray, to accompany the

air spray with the verbal command "no" and follow it with lots of affection when the bad behavior stops.

Above all, keep yourself cheerfully determined to consistently discipline your cat. When you cannot supervise him, see that he is in an area where he cannot do damage. This isolation is not punishment for your cat, it is a deterrent to further damage to your home and a means of keeping the pet from developing or reinforcing a bad habit.

With this in mind, remember to give your little friend lots of love and affection when you release him from his confined area. *With a combination of love and consistent discipline, you can have loving cats and a lovely home.*

INSOMNIAC CATS

At one time or another, all kittens have problems with nighttime wakefulness. By this I mean both cat and owner are awake, but on the owner's part, it is not by choice.

Kittens and cats have a tremendous amount of energy. They also express a wide range of emotions: affection, rage, indifference, sadness and happiness. They are all demonstrated at one time or another. Sometimes the cat's energy level is accelerated by anxiety and stress, which often makes him restless and prevents good sleeping habits.

All cats, when left alone, will sleep the greater part of the day and be awake and playful in the evening. It's easy to change his pattern of eat-sleep-play if we are at home during the day and take the time to reinforce a daytime-play, nighttime-sleep schedule.

Many of us, busy or away during the day, don't notice what bad habits our cats are falling into until we are awakened in the middle of the night with kitty nibbling on our ears, punching us in the stomach, or playfully digging under the blankets.

We, in return, push the cat away while mumbling dire predictions about his future health—only to encounter a fresh assault because the cat naturally assumes that we are also playing! From here on, the battle becomes stronger as we try to convince the playful darling that we are not amused and don't wish to play at 3:00 A.M. Isolating the cat in another room is successful only for the few owners who can sleep through any yowl, or who own houses large enough to remove the pet to some place out of earshot.

While a cat is one of the easiest pets to have around, all living creatures do require some time and attention. If your schedule forces you to be away for many hours, leaving the cat to sleep during your absence, you will need to teach him to adjust to your living habits.

Of course, cats do resist change, but this is not a change, it's merely an adjustment which should not cause any stress-induced temperamental outbursts. In fact, you are the one feeling the stress, so you have an added incentive for finding the time to reverse your pet's sleep pattern.

Remember, your cat will be happiest if you establish and follow a set routine. If you are more than a few minutes late with your cat's regularly scheduled meal, be prepared to get a good bawling out before he condescends to eat your offering. On such occassions, I have found that apologizing at the top of my voice as I enter the kitchen and quickly prepare the cat's meal leaves my feline too surprised to be angry.

Since cats doze anywhere from 18 to 20 hours a day, you will need to offer some daytime entertainment to help him remain alert during your hours away from home. A window for your pet to view the world is the easiest entertainment available. Since he is naturally curious, viewing the outside world is a great delight.

Provide a few toys which he enjoys and change the playthings once or twice a week to keep your cat from becoming bored. A strong scratching post with a toy swinging from it will amuse him for quite a while. A paper bag left on the floor with a ping-pong ball inside is sheer delight for any playful feline.

Once you have set the new household schedule and decide to follow it conscientiously, you should return home each evening, reasonably close to dinner time. Once home, take a few minutes to give your pet the attention he has been waiting for. Talking, petting and scratching the ears and tummy help to soothe him and put him in a playful mood.

Your actions during the early evening hours will mean the difference in whether your cat sleeps all night or wakes up refreshed and ready to play before morning's light. There is no other way to keep his schedule the same as yours, except to keep kitty awake for at least two hours before bedtime. This is not as difficult as it may seem. With a little planning, your new schedule will be established within a short time.

EXERCISE—INSIDE/OUTSIDE

Although the cat that never goes outside alone is safe, he will need more of your attention to help him work off excess energy. During nice weather, you might try taking him outside on a harness and lengthy lightweight cord.

With your cat confined in a harness, you can sit in the yard and allow him to sniff, roll and play safely while you doze or read. Playing fetch with a piece of crumpled paper can also be done outside. This provides strenuous exercise for the pet, but requires little effort on your part.

Living in an apartment can be an exciting life for any cat, if you schedule a daily walk through the halls, down to the laundry room, or to visit a neighbor in the same building. Kitty will always find new and interesting sights, sounds and objects, even if the same route is covered each evening.

Evening play for the household feline is also a pleasure for you, the owner. After all, you own a cat for your enjoyment and your cat feels he owns you for his enjoyment—so enjoy! Play chase with a sash, ribbon or cord. Urge him to fetch with any round soft ball. Cut a hole in a large grocery bag and after the cat runs into the bag, dangle your fingers or a cord through the hole for him to snatch.

Hold and play with your cat. Satisfy his boundless energy. You will both be tired as bedtime approaches, and I guarantee that you and your pet will get a good night's rest.

DAYTIME/NIGHTTIME SCHEDULE

Assuming that you work in the daytime, try this system on Friday evening and see if you can get a good schedule started by Monday morning.

Feed your cats Friday morning before leaving for work and upon returning in the evening. From this day on, feed your cats their regular meals in the morning and at night. After this have snacks available at all times. If the cats become hungry between meals they can nibble on the snacks. Dry tidbits are adequate.

During the evening hours keep the cats awake by playing, petting and entertaining them. You will get tired, but don't allow the cats to sleep until you go to bed. If they wish to go out-of-doors during the early evening, or if you think it's a good time for their outside exercise, put the cats outside and ignore their pleas to come back inside until you think it's time. You are now establishing a comfortable routine for both you and your cats.

During your sleeping hours, put your cats in an area as far away from your bedroom as possible. Be sure they have their snacks, water, and litter box with them. Now begins the battle of endurance. Since you have given in to your cats so often, they will undoubtedly yell and scratch at the door. Cats rather enjoy this type of battle and can show amazing determination. You, on the other hand, will soon become tired, and wish to give up the battle. **Don't do it!** Your cats are fed, warm and have all they need for a comfortable night. It will not take too many nights before they give up and sleep. In the morning, feed and play with them before you leave the house. Of course they will sleep while you are gone. It's too bad you will not be able to do the same. If the cats have a window to watch the world's activities, they might stay awake a little more, but don't count on it.

Here are a few added suggestions:

Never feed your cats except at their morning and evening meal time and continue providing the nutritious snacks. Do not, under any circumstances, get up in the night for the cats unless you have to use discipline. They must learn to leave you alone to sleep. A few months from now, if the cats have adjusted to their new schedule, you may allow them to sleep with you, but only if the cats follow your rules. During retraining when the cats yell and scratch so much you are a wreck, open their door and spray or pour water on them. At the same time say "no!" and immediately close the door.

If you really stick to this routine—and it will be hard for you—your cats will eventually adjust. Soon you and your feline pals will start a new and loving relationship, based on mutual respect.

PART 3

Penny Pinching Home Health Care

LOOKING GOOD—GROOMING

Your cat's fur is made for outdoor living. It protects the skin from sun rays, extreme cold, dampness, and helps to regulate the cat's body temperature. The double (under and outer) fur coat provides the insulation which helps the feline's body adjust to extremes in temperature with ease and comfort. In fact, your cat's coat is his health barometer.

While outdoor cats shed seasonally, those kept indoors shed year-round. It's easy to see when your long-haired pet is shedding. The loose hair quickly covers furniture, rugs and clothing. Shorthaired cats shed just as much as those with long hair, but unless the color of your furniture and carpets contrast with his hair color, you may not notice.

Since most feline's sweat glands are in the feet, the skin does not secrete moisture to keep the coat in good condition. When a cat grooms himself, nature provides the moisture necessary for a healthy coat.

There are several reasons for helping our pets with grooming chores. If a cat, especially a long-haired one, does all his own grooming, he can swallow an excessive amount of hair. The hair then forms a ball in the stomach that becomes a dangerous obstruction, interfering with his digestive system.

FIRST AID FOR HAIRBALLS

Even if your cat is never bothered with hairballs, he is certain to be more comfortable if you help him keep his coat free of dirt, mats and parasites. Your family will be happier, too, with clean air to breathe, hair-free clothes, and carpeting without fleas.

To help prevent hairballs, many cat owners feed their pets wheat germ oil or a commercial coat conditioner. Your cat will like the taste of most of these products, but if he objects, there is a simple way to give the medicine to him. Just squeeze the paste onto your index finger and rub it behind the cat's lower front teeth. It is unlikely that he will be able to spit out the medicine because it sticks to the roof of his mouth and his teeth.

If dandruff is a persistent problem, dry air is probably the cause. Adding moisture to the air in your home will help prevent dry hair and flaking dandruff. It will also minimize the static electricity that often bothers both you and your pet. An occasional application of one of the protein coat conditioners available for felines will also keep the coat sweet smelling and healthy.

Most cats enjoy being brushed, if grooming is started while they're kittens, and is made a pleasant routine. A grooming session can be a special time that allows both you and your kit to have fun together and show one another affection.

If your adult cat does not enjoy being brushed, you can still do this by wrapping him in a towel or putting him into a mesh bag that allows you to expose only the area of the body that you are brushing.

Cats seldom if ever need a bath. When a bath is necessary, place a piece of carpeting or a heavy towel in the bottom of the sink to give him a firm grip. Use a shampoo made for felines, then wash him starting from the neck and moving down to the tail. Go back and wash the head last. If the cat is uncontrollable, put him in a mesh bag and wash one part at a time.

REMOVING TANGLES—GROOMING TOOLS

Every long-haired cat occasionally gets mats and tangles. To help with these problems, you may wish to try a commercial prepared detangler product. If you don't have one on hand when you need it, here's a simple home remedy that has always worked well for our pets.

Begin by rubbing mineral, cooking or wheat germ oil into the tangles. Allow the oil to set for a short time and carefully work the tangles free with your fingers. Finish by combing the area with first a wide-tooth then a fine-tooth comb. Once the mats and tangles are gone, shampoo the spot and rinse carefully. Your cat may get a little feisty before you finish this treatment, but most will submit without a battle if only a small area is involved.

A spot shampoo, followed by a thorough rinse with a wet

71

towel, is also an effective and easy way to keep the hair around the ears and tail free from oil. After rinsing the spot, rub the cat's entire coat with the clean wet towel. Finish with a good brushing to leave the coat tangle-free, clean and shiny.

A few years ago, I found another grooming aid that I use on both cats and dogs. It seemed that the hair around the pets' outer ears was often oily and messy looking because of the cleanser I used to keep their inner ears clean and free of parasites. Now I prefer an acne pad or commercial feline ear solution to treat their inner ears leaving the surface hair clean and free of oil.

Good-quality tools make grooming easier and more comfortable for both you and your cat. Natural bristle brushes cost a little more, but they are far superior to nylon. Wash them often to remove oil. Medium-width steel combs with round, smooth teeth protect a fine coat and won't hurt sensitive skin. A soft toothbrush makes removing dark eye stains easy, and a soft shoe polish brush is great on the cat's face, around the ears, and between toes.

Attachments for animal care, now available with some vacuum cleaners, are new and useful grooming tools. These provide a wonderful way to remove loose hair from both cats and dogs; but you have to accustom your pets to the noise and suction while they are still young.

Pick a time when your kitten is content and sleepy to hold him and rub the vacuum nozzle attachment, power off, over his body. Repeat this often till your pet is familiar with the feel of the nozzle.

Next, turn on the vacuum motor, but keep it far away from the kitten at first, giving him time to become familiar with the noise. Gradually move it closer. If you take your time, the cat will eventually become comfortable with the vacuum noise and find pleasure in the gentle rubbing on his coat.

I have trained all my pets to enjoy being vacuumed. My family and pets both recommend this marvelous and comfortable grooming aid.

CARE OF THE EARS

All cats scratch their ears occasionally, but when you see him scratch continually, you'll know he has a problem. It could be a simple case of fleas, or in the autumn, scratching may be caused by allergies.

The most common reason for scratching among household pets is a small invisible mite called otodectes cynotis, or the common ear mite. This mite causes discomfort, restlessness and often severe pain.

Ear mites are easily detected by dark discharge, reddened skin and the obvious discomfort of your cat. Mites are constant travelers and one of the few parasites that cat and dog transmit to each other. In fact, kittens are often infected soon after birth by the mother cat. When you find ear mites on one household pet you should check all others and begin treatment on the infected animals.

Ear mites will not go away without treatment. The mite will breed more larvae and inflame and damage the surrounding inner ear tissue. The infection will become worse as the tormented pet scratches and further bruises the tender skin.

If you have not encountered mites before, take your cat to the vet for a proper diagnoses. He or she will check a sample under a microscope for white specks, about the size of the head of a pin, which move.

Do not attempt any treatment until you have a proper diagnosis. Once you have treated ear mites, you will have no trouble identifying them. When you are certain the cat is infected by mites again, you can then ask the vet for the medicine without an office call.

HOW TO APPLY EAR MEDICINE

Most ear medicine comes in long-nozzled tubes, which are inserted into the ear canal before releasing the medicine. Wrap your cat in a towel or have a partner hold him tight while medicating so the tip will not damage the delicate skin of the inner ear. Squeeze the medicine into the ear and gently rub the outer surface to help the liquid work deep into the ear canal. Massage the broad, lower part of the ear near the head until you hear a squishy sound. You will then know the application has been effectively completed.

FLEAS—FLEA COLLARS

Did you know that one little flea will bite your cat on the average of 25 times in one hour? Two fleas mean twice the discomfort, and you can just imagine the havoc a whole family of fleas can wreak in just a short time upon your unsuspecting feline.

The flea's constant movement and biting cause itching and irritation that can make your pet so uncomfortable, he will be unable to rest. In addition, flea bites and the scratching they prompt can cause infections that require expensive treatment.

Since the flea lives on blood, a severe flea infestation can cause a pet to suffer from anemia, and cause weight loss and generally deteriorating health.

If fleas weren't such dangerous and irritating little critters, one could almost admire their ability to survive. Fleas breed anywhere and everywhere. They love carpets and can survive and breed in the deep pile all year round. Outside, the yard and garden are also perfect breeding spots. Even if you never allow your pets outside, fleas will find their way to them. They can travel inside on your clothing or simply invade your home through open doors and screened windows.

In warmer climates, fleas are a constant problem, while only the hardiest of fleas can survive the cold weather in the northern states. Regardless of where you live, after only a few weeks of warm weather, the flea population literally explodes. That's why flea control should start early in the summer and continue through the warm fall months, even in the cold winter states.

Effective flea control includes removing the insects from both the animal and his environment. In fact, it's cruel to allow your household pets out of doors in the summer without adequate protection from flea infestation.

Spraying gardens and adjacent property with a good yard and kennel spray and repeating the treatment as often as directed on the container, is one effective flea control method. But one weapon alone will not win the war. It's also necessary to use either a flea spray or flea powder routinely, or put a flea collar on your cat. If you have more than one pet, each must be treated simultaneously, since fleas can easily jump from one pet to the other.

You can increase the effectiveness of a spray or powder by wrapping your pet in a large blanket or towel for about 20 minutes after applying the insecticide. This cover will insure that the fleas don't jump off the animal before the poison has a chance to work. Do take care, however, to protect the pet's nose and eyes from the insecticide and keep his or her face open to fresh air during the treatment. When you remove the wrapping, you may be surprised at the number of dead fleas you'll find on the cover and on the animal's fur.

It's almost impossible to control fleas in most areas without the help of insecticides; but if you treat the environment—spray the yard, the carpets and furniture in your home—you may be able to avoid using these chemicals directly on the pet. Regular use of a flea comb may be all the extra protection your friend will need. A few pet owners have reported some success with the use of brewer's yeast, or tablets containing brewer's yeast, as a means of repelling fleas. Frequent vacuuming, paying particular attention to corners and areas along the baseboards, is another nonpoisonous method of flea control. Be sure to discard the dust bag frequently to keep it from becoming just another breeding ground for these hardy pests.

Certainly, the most popular method of flea control is the flea collar. Collars are convenient, comparatively inexpensive and effective when used correctly; but there are a few potential dangers you should guard against.

The flea collar is damp when the package is first opened. Leave the collar in the opened package until it's dry—usually two days. Avoid touching the damp collar.

Once the collar is dry, wipe the excess powder off the collar before placing it around the cat's neck and be sure to wash your hands after handling it.

The collar should be loose enough to allow you to slide two fingers between it and the pet's neck, but not so loose that the cat can slide it up and into his mouth. (This can happen and usually results in a very sick pet!)

Check the cat's skin underneath the collar periodically for any signs of skin irritation. If any redness or rash appears, remove the collar at once and consult your veterinarian.

Cut off the extra length of collar. If your pet chews on the dangling end, he may show signs of poisoning, such as vomiting, diarrhea and convulsions.

Do not wrap a collar around your cat's neck more than once even if it is long enough to allow this.

Do not put a flea collar on a very young pet. Kittens and puppies should be at least 12 weeks old before wearing a flea collar.

Do not use a dog flea collar on a cat. Use only collars made specifically made for cats.

Do not use a flea collar in combination with other insecticides, such as shampoos, dips or powders—unless the procedure is recommended by your veterinarian.

Avoid touching the collar to your skin when you handle the cat. Human skin may sometimes react to the insecticide, producing a rash that can last up to 90 days.

Hopefully, these suggestions will help both you and your pets enjoy a happy, flea-free, healthy summer.

SHOPPING FOR A VETERINARIAN

Most cat owners are as genuinely concerned about choosing a good veterinarian as they are about choosing a good family practitioner. It's wise to start your pet with a veterinarian while he is very young because your pet should receive all necessary inoculations and at least one checkup each year.

How should you choose a veterinarian? What makes one vet better than another? Is a good personality important?

Here are some practical tips for pet owners:

The easiest and most direct method of finding the best vet for you is to talk about it with friends and acquaintances. You may also write to your State Veterinarian Medical Association for a list of animal doctors in your area.

Most reputable veterinarians are members of their state

association and can take advantage of the educational courses offered. This helps them keep up to date with the latest developments in their field.

Once you have chosen a vet, make a visit to the office. One visit will tell many things. Are the facilities and staff clean? Is everyone helpful and kind in handling your cat? Do they really listen to what you have to say and honestly try to answer your questions? Is someone available day and night for an emergency? Are they willing to discuss the cost of specific services such as worming, neutering and shots?

Animal doctors may specialize in large and small animals, which would include horses and cows, or they may provide service to only small animals. Some vets specialize in a particular medical field such as dermatology, radiology or opthalmology.

Any reputable veterinarian will send clients to a specialist when necessary. In return, you should also feel free to consult another doctor if you are uncomfortable with the diagnosis or treatment of your pet. Please have the courtesy of talking your concern over with your vet before going to another doctor.

Occasionally you may be upset about the treatment, or worse, the death of your pet. If you feel that your veterinarian has behaved in an unethical or unscrupulous manner, you may inform your State Board of Veterinary Medicine which will investigate the situation. This is a serious step and should not be taken lightly. You should give yourself time to calm down, get over your grief and once again talk to your vet before considering such a measure.

Happily with proper exercise, good nutrition and loving care, most of us have pets who live long lives and maintain good health with only a yearly visit to a veterinarian.

TIMING CRUCIAL FOR CALLING VET

Knowing when to take your cat to the veterinarian is one of the most perplexing problems for the average owner.

If I take my pet to the doctor at the beginning of an illness, I am usually told that it's a little early to tell.

If I wait and take the cat when he is really sick, I'm told that I just made it, but with a little luck and a great deal of skill he might survive.

Tiring of this type of hit or miss diagnosis I have developed a list of "hurry to the vet" symptoms that I have found useful:

BREATHING DIFFICULTY: If the cat has been exercising vigorously, labored breathing is normal. If the cat frequently gasps for breath or pants after a short exertion, you should be concerned. Your pet might have foreign matter in the lungs, an allergy or respiratory disease. Shortness of breath may be a result of insufficient oxygen to the heart. Distemper, severe anemia or broken ribs all create a demand for more air. Don't wait! Take your cat to the vet immediately.

RUNNY EYES: If this is the only symptom the cat has, wash out his eyes twice a day with cotton balls and sterile water. Unless the eyes become bloodshot or have pus in the corners, I don't worry about the cat; the eyes usually clear in a few days. If pus or other signs of illness develop with the eye problem, of course you must find out what the trouble is.

80

COUGHING: This is always serious enough to stay alert. If a cough persists for more than two days you must get the cat to a vet immediately. Coughing is nature's way of clearing the respiratory passages of obstruction. A cough could be a symptom of an allergy, pneumonia, hair balls or an obstruction in the throat. Coughing should never be ignored.

VOMITING: Many people are so disgusted and angry with this unpleasant act that they forget that vomiting is a symptom of intestinal disorder. A light cold, eating spoiled food, or a stomach obstruction are among reasons the stomach rejects food. I usually stop all food for 24 hours if one of my cats has a stomach upset. After 24 hours I give a very light meal and see if the cat retains the food. If he vomits again it is best to call the vet and discuss the problem.

SNEEZING: When sneezing is the only symptom I observe, I usually assume my cat has run into something she is allergic to. Unless the sneezing continues for more than a day, I ignore the whole thing. If the reaction is severe you should get some medicine for the cat's relief.

ACCIDENTS: Any time my cat is hit by a car, even if he gets up and seems to feel fine, I have him checked by the veterinarian. Internal injuries do not always develop immediately.

DIARRHEA: This is such a common complaint that we may overlook the fact that it is dangerous, especially in kittens, if not checked. Diarrhea can result from something as simple as a change in diet or an emotional upset. It can also be the symptom of serious illness, such as internal parasites, poisoning or infection. It may even precede the common cold. Whatever the cause, help must be found as soon as possible. If the stools do not return to normal after two days of a bland diet, take the cat to a veterinarian.

FEVER: A warm, dry nose is not a sign of fever. The only accurate way to find out if your cat has a fever is to take its temperature. A normal reading for a cat is about 101 to 102.5 degrees Fahrenheit. Watch for further signs of illness, and consult your veterinarian.

BAD BREATH: This is a common complaint, especially with older cats who are having problems with teeth. You should periodically check the cat's teeth and gums thoroughly. If they appear healthy, you need to look elsewhere for the solution.

Quite often, mouth odor originates in the stomach or intestinal tract. The problem could be simple indigestion, and a change of food could stop the odor. If the odor persists, I usually give my cat a little charcoal, available in pet stores. It is supposed to aid digestion. Many times, bad breath is hard to diagnose. If you cannot find the answer within a reasonable time, take your cat to the veterinarian for a good checkup.

CONVULSIONS: These frightening episodes are always a symptom of some problem. They could be caused by something as simple as an ear infection or as severe as poisoning, distemper, brain damage or heart trouble. A call to the vet is in order.

As a whole, common sense tells us when to go to the veterinarian and when to try a few simple home remedies. When in doubt, a call to the veterinarian may save hours of needless worry.

HOW TO GIVE MEDICINE

Since even the bravest cat owner quakes at the thought of giving their reluctant feline medicine, here are some methods you may try until you find the easiest and most effective application for both you and your cat.

The quick push: Place the cat on your lap and calmly pet and sooth him while you place your hand on his head, with your fingers pointing forward. With the palm of your hand against the back of his head, quickly wrap your fingers around until you press the joints at the corners of the cat's mouth. With the thumb and index finger open the mouth. As it is forced open, elevate his head and tighten your hold. With the other hand push the pill as far down the cat's throat as possible. After inserting the pill, hold the mouth closed and slightly tilt the cat's head until he swallows. Stroking the throat downward or blowing gently into the nose will hasten the pill's descent.

When you use the "quick push" you must work fast. It takes a little practice to complete the action before your cat has time to resist. Many people use this method with great success, but it is best accomplished when the cat is in a relaxed mood and the pill is injected quickly.

Crushing the pill and adding the contents to your cat's favorite food is a simple task, but most felines with their persnickety taste and fantastic sense of smell, refuse to touch it.

There is a commercial pill pusher available in pet supply stores which works well, once you become accustomed to using it. The pusher looks like a large plastic syringe and the action is the same as an injection. The tip, which goes into the cat's mouth, is soft and the unit is non-breakable. You may find, upon trying, this inexpensive method of pill pushing is convenient for you and non-irritating to your cat.

Giving liquid medicine with a plastic eye dropper is by far the most comfortable for both you and your cat. Find a time when he is sleepy and content then gently pull the skin at the side of his lower jaw out far enough to insert the dropper tip and release the medication into the side of the cheek. Tilt the cat's head back so the liquid will flow down the throat. If you do this quickly, the cat will hardly notice.

Since many cats accept liquid medication with fewer battles, ask your veterinarian if the medicine your pet needs is available in liquid form. If not, find out if the pill may be crushed and added to a liquid without altering the effectiveness.

CORRECT FINICKY EATER'S HABITS

All cats should have healthy appetites and eat a well balanced diet. When there is more than one animal in the family you usually have no problem; however, a cat raised alone may get spoiled. If you have a fussy eater, you can stop all of that nonsense and change your pet into a happy eager eater, with the following system.

Check with your veterinarian to be sure that your cat has no internal parasites. If he is in good health, find a convenient food that contains nutritious ingredients and is pleasant tasting.

Now the hard part—you must forbid your cat all food for twenty-four hours. Not even a scrap should be given. This system may be hard on you if you have children in the family giving the cat snacks, but you are doing this for his health, so you must be firm.

After twenty-four hours have passed, put one-fourth of your cat's normal amount of food in a dish, put it down and leave the room. Twenty or thirty minutes later, return and remove the dish whether your cat has eaten the food or not. Until the food is completely eaten, continue this schedule.

When the cat eagerly eats up the food, you may increase the amount by another quarter at the next feeding. It may take only a few days or as long as a week or two before the cat is ready for a larger amount of food. Don't be discouraged, he will eventually eat. In fact, you may have been overfeeding the pet, so increase by quarter amounts

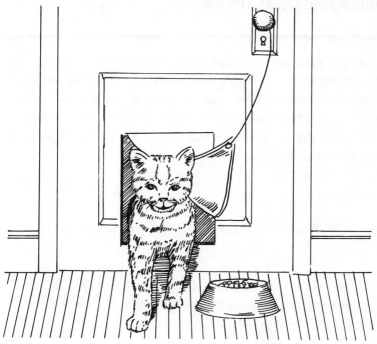

only when he has completely eaten the last meal. Remember, don't feed your cat between meals until his appetite has improved.

Many cattery's feed their cats a well balanced dry kibble. It's convenient and less expensive to serve dry kibbles, and if your cat prefers, the food may be moistened with meat broth, milk, or water. Chewing dry food aids in keeping your cat's teeth clean and provides all necessary nutrition.

When your cat is eagerly eating its food reduce one-half of one meal, once a week. This system of refusing food may sound extreme but remember, you will have a happy eater because you loved your cat enough to be concerned about its health.

QUICK APPETIZERS FOR YOUR PET

Once your cat is eating well and may occasionally be rewarded with a treat, try our family pets' favorite crunchy munchy cookies. This healthy snack is so easy to make that even a pre-teenager can manage alone. The recipe is sufficient for a cat or a small dog. I double or triple the ingredients for gift giving.

CRUNCHY MUNCHIES FOR CATS AND DOGS

Mix one 3½ ounce jar of strained meat baby food, four heaping teaspoons of powdered non-fat milk, and six heaping teaspoons of wheat germ.

Shape the dough into small balls, roll in wheat germ or flour and flatten slightly with a fork. If you find the ingredients too dry to handle comfortably, add a little meat broth or water.

Bake on a greased cookie sheet until brown and dry, in a 350 degree oven. This takes about 30 minutes. If you double the recipe and make larger cookies, increase the baking time according to the size.

Crunchy munchies are dry, hard, and excellent for keeping your pet's teeth clean. They also make great gifts when given in a decorative, air tight container, with a bow on top.

BALANCED DIET FOR FAT OR THIN

If your cat is so plump that his ribs cannot be felt through the fat, it's time to put your friend on a diet. Overweight cats tend to have shorter lives and more problems with their health. The most common ailments fat cats suffer are heart disease, arthritis, and respiratory illness.

Growing kittens under one year of age, need twice the amount of protein that adult cats require. To keep your pet slim, trim, and healthy, you should feed your older cat fewer calories as he ages.

If your cat is fed an all meat diet, whether fresh, frozen, or canned, he is probaby getting too much fat. Although cats do need protein in some form, they do not require meat for a well-balanced daily ration.

There are many canned cat foods on the market which have supplements to provide the added nutrients needed for a balanced diet. If you insist on canned meat for your cat, read the labels until you find a food with the proper proportions of protein, carbohydrates, and fat.

Vegetable protein soy products are a valuable low-fat diet supplement for cats with special nutrition requirements. If you feel your cat needs a special, or low-fat diet, consult your veterinarian.

The individual meal size packets of food, now available in all flavors to suit the most fastidious taste, are certainly convenient. They do not require refrigeration and are so handy that I usually switch all my family pets to these carefree packets when we travel. Individual packets of food vary in content and flavor, so shop around for the best quality at a reasonable price. High priced foods don't seem expensive when you have a single pet, but both canned and individual packets of food can become high priced when your family pets increase.

A normal cat that does not need a special diet will grow and stay healthy when fed a well-balanced dry commercial food. You may serve kibbles either moistened with milk, canned meats, or with added table scraps. My cats enjoy eating kibbles as they come from the bag with nothing added. Of course there is a large bowl of water beside the food at all times.

Dry kibbles not only provide a complete diet, they also help to prevent dental tartar and promote healthy teeth and gums.

When you feed your cat, allow him 20 to 30 minutes to eat and then remove the dish. This is plenty of time for your eager eater to finish the meal. Throw away any food left in the dish and do not feed your cat again until the next scheduled meal.

Any cat that needs to lose weight must have his daily calories reduced. This is easily accomplished by cutting the amount of food offered by one-fourth. The reduced amount of food may be given twice a day to help your cat escape hunger pains.

Give your cat only low calorie snacks while he is on a diet. You are being tough because you want your beloved pet to live a long and healthy life.

EMOTIONALLY DISTURBED STRAY CATS

A week ago a stray cat was dumped off at my door. It's not the first time this has occurred. Maybe he was meant for one of the neighbors, or maybe someone just dumped him and hoped he would find a good home. Worst of all, some child may be crying for this well-cared for, affectionate half-grown cat. I tried in every way I knew to find the cat's home and owners.

Frustrated, I decided to talk to my young cat-loving neighbor down the street. I met Cheryl Hoyle a few years ago when I walked by her old stately farmhouse located right in the middle of a city block. The large yard, not beautiful by people standards but neat and clean, has lots of grass and a few very old oak trees that shed their abundant large leaves early in the fall. I was first attracted to Cheryl's home on a day in late autumn when I saw a half-dozen cats playfully diving under the dry leaves. The cats seemed carefree and fun-loving until I tried to approach them, but dashed for cover as I drew near.

Cheryl, a Mathematics teacher in a local high school and a very independent lady, came out and talked about her cats. As a collector of stray cats, she ranks among the best because her cats cannot be placed with a family. They live in a special world of fear and uncertainty. "You must make stray cats adopt you," confides Cheryl. "Many times it takes months and often the cat that has been too neglected or misused can never become confident of your affection."

As Cheryl continued, I tried to see into one of the two wooden cat houses which stood side by side on the front porch. "That's Arthur," said Cheryl. "He is a truly quirky cat. When he came here most of his bottom teeth were gone, one eye had cornea damage and was all cloudy and no one could get near him. He was a fighter and all of the other cats ran from him. I fed him," she continued, "for six months before I could get a good look at him. He needed medical care and it's hard to stay calm and wait, but there is little else you can do.

I put food out for Arthur every morning and evening. He was always waiting and would come and sit at a distance, until I had put the food down and gone back inside of the house. Each feeding poor Arthur would eat and then run away to hide. But I had to wait for my stray cat to adopt me," she exclaimed again as she leaned down and stretched a loving hand to scratch Arthur. "It was a year before I could touch this boy and gain his trust. He still will not live in the house or with the other cats but the fire is gone and he is enjoying old age."

STRAYS MUST FIND WATER

Few people realize that cats need drinking water and many times cannot find it. Most stray cats will not eat snow and suffer continually from lack of their most basic necessity—water. Cheryl puts buckets of warm water near the back door year-round. Warm water many times helps comfort the stray, plus warm water will remain free of ice longer. In cold weather, she also heats the milk given daily to the strays.

When a stray shows up in the Hoyle yard, Cheryl puts extra food and water in a secluded area to tempt the cat to eat. Since much of the stress a stray cat feels is 'where is my next meal coming from' this first communication with food is the most important contact. Along with the stress of finding food, Cheryl knows that the cat is thinking, 'can I trust anyone?'

Jud came into the Hoyle yard one day and stayed. Since he was an agreeable cat, Cheryl easily caught him and went to the vet to have him neutered, as soon as she could. Jud came home, well and happy and immediately disappeared. Six months later he showed up at her door again. He still shows up occasionally but obviously has other homes. "You just take a stray cat on its terms," sighed Cheryl. "You can't bathe them or fuss over them. Many times it takes weeks just to get near enough to take care of the noticeable wounds they have. Of course, I always try to catch the strays and have them neutered, but sometimes even that is impossible. The rewards are there though," she said. "Even though it's not necessary, once in a while one of my cats stops fighting the world, and turns to lick the hand that feeds it. I treasure those moments."

What should you do when you notice a stray cat in your yard? Your first objective is to offer food and water to the cat. If at all possible, look the cat over without touching and see whether it needs medical help. After the cat has eaten, provide a bed in a secluded area such as a garage or tool shed. *Don't bring the stray into the house among your household pets until it is examined by a veterinarian.*

The cat may be sick or infected with parasites, which can be transmitted to your home and inhabitants.

Don't try to touch the cat if it is frightened. You must let the stray develop confidence in you at its own pace. Never rush at a stray cat or it may leave your area. As time passes, watch the cat for indications of trust. When you feel the time is right, offer some tasty food from your hand. As your hand feeding progresses, you will eventually find the proper time to reach out and carefully pet your little friend.

Since eating and sleeping are a cats main occupation, do as Cheryl suggests and give your stray a variety of foods. Dry kibbles which take longer to eat are desirable, with alternate meals of semi-moist and canned food. Milk is optional, but most stray cats enjoy this treat. Always keep fresh water near the sleeping area.

What are the stresses that control a stray cat's life?

Trusting—can I trust anyone? If I do will they suddenly turn on me?

Food and Shelter—will it always be available and safe?

External Enemies—must I be careful of other cats, dogs, cars and people?

Illness—where can I safely hide when I am sick and hurt?

How much easier it is to be patient with the homeless cat when we are aware of its problems. It is also easier to understand why many stray cats, even though they are well cared for, pace about the house crying for no apparent reason. Many of them remain restless for the remainder of their lives.

HOW TO PLACE A STRAY CAT

Certainly a neutered cat is more easily placed in a new home. If you find the cost prohibitive, contact your local animal shelter or humane society. They may have help for homeless pets and their owners. Most potential owners find having a neutered pet offered is far more desirable than assuming the cost themselves.

Have confidence in the potential owner of your stray cat and tell him/her of any daily problems which might reoccur. Most cat lovers can handle the cat's stress if prepared ahead.

Many laundromats, cleaners and corner stores will place a small announcement to help you find a new owner. If you include a picture of the cat, you may get a faster response.

A cleverly worded, short ad in the local newspaper is worth the money. Spreading the news through friends and acquaintances is also helpful. Meanwhile, until you find a home which will be beneficial for your stray cat, continue your loving care. He trusts you.

CHANGING ENVIRONMENT MAY CAUSE STRESS

I don't remember ever moving to another city without toting at least two cats along with the family. Those were the good ol' days, when cat owners simply got along as well as they could, trying earnestly to help their felines adjust to their new territory. Many cats, lacking the freedom to choose their environment when moved, disappeared at the first opportunity and became strays, or found new homes.

Fortunately today we have the opportunity to understand our cat's emotions and the resulting stress involved when they are forced to change their surroundings. By understanding, we have the ability to help our felines adjust to the new environment, without prolonged separation anxiety.

Indoor cats usually find adapting their daily routine to new surroundings much easier than outdoor cats. Of course, those living indoors must re-route their daily exercise pattern along a new household path; but they can keep their eating and grooming habits intact.

Outdoor cats when relocated face as many new situations as a new kid in the neighborhood. Hostile strangers and unfamiliar territory can certainly disturb and frighten the normally easy-going feline. Panicked by the forced change, the cat may become nervous, fearful, and finally anti-social.

Cats, of all domestic animals, are without a doubt the most rigid about their routines. No red-blooded feline would put up with the casual schedules forced upon dogs by their owners. Upon coming home exhausted and late from an important appointment, we are promptly punished for our cat's delayed dinner by being snubbed or yelled at.

Dogs, on the other hand, greet us cheerfully, thankful that we show up at all. *It is easy to see that dogs, the most people-oriented of all household pets, adjust to new surroundings more easily than cats, the most self-oriented of all family pets.*

There are many "if possible" activities that you, the

owner, can do to ease your pet into a new home and territory.

If possible:

TRAIN YOUR CAT to ride in the car before you take him on the long trip to your new home.

TAKE YOUR CAT with you to visit your new living quarters several times before the actual move. He will probably enjoy sniffing around the empty rooms. When the permanent move is made, he will remember the territory and relax.

ARRANGE THE FURNITURE in your new home the same as in the old house. Your cat may then follow many of the rituals he has set for his daily routine without too much interference. After a few months, the furniture may be moved; but as expected, he will either love or hate the new arrangement.

PUT THE CAT'S food, litter box and other accouterments in approximately the same place in your new living areas.

SINCE SMELLING IS our cat's most important method of identification, bringing the everyday smells of the old home into the new home can help. The same personal odors that pervade the bedroom, bath, kitchen and living room can easily be distributed through the new home with little difficulty. In fact, to prevent future litter box problems, check the flooring in your new home for old urine stains, and clean the area thoroughly with a strong deodorizer.

ON THE DAY, it's important to keep your cat confined. Both indoor and outdoor cats should be kept in the house or several days before the move. A cat can ense when change is in the air; and if allowed outside, he may depart to hide. If you keep kitty in the house, you'll know he will be there when you look for him. Give him extra love and reassurance when you can. Try to stay calm during this stressful time.

ON MOVING DAY don't carry the cat in your arms out to the car. A sudden noise can panic even the calmest feline, provoking a quick jump from your arms. Put him on his leash or in a secure box. Once inside the car, keep him close to you to pat and assure him that all is well.

When you have arrived at your new dwelling, lock your cat in a room to prevent him from slipping outside while the doors are open. Place his litter box and dishes in the same room and allow him to relax while he explores this part of his new home.

An outdoor cat should be kept indoors for at least one week after moving. During this time, he becomes familiar with the new neighborhood as he watches the activities through the windows. Daily walks on a harness and leash will help your pet to get acquainted with the neighbors and live in harmony with both humans and animals.

LITTER BOX CARE

Cleanliness is a vital concern to all cat owners, and good litter box habits are necessary for a happy home. Provide your kitten with a litter box large enough to be comfortable and contains space for the kitten to do a little wild scratching. All cat owners soon learn that cats occasionally get into their litter boxes just to scratch up a storm. Excess energy? Only your cat knows. Regardless, you must be prepared for litter all over the floor if the box is not large enough for your cat's antics. Besides scratching, many cats enjoy sleeping in their litter boxes instead of the beautiful beds we provide. I usually try to discourage this, but with cats you can't win all the time. Most cats, luxury lovers that they are, will eventually seek a softer bed.

Your cat may refuse to use his box because the litter is not changed often enough. The strong odor of urine ammonia discourages him, and in desperation he will use the floor.

If you line the litter pan with two thick layers of newspaper, the papers will absorb much of the urine and the litter will remain dry. You may also use one of the new padded liners available in your pet supply section. Add about 4 inches of litter on top of the papers, and when the top layer gets wet, slip it out and throw it away. This will keep the litter dry and odor-free longer.

When cleaning the litter box, remove the urine-soiled newspapers and place them in a plastic garbage bag together with the soiled litter. Tie up the bag and you have a water-proof, easy-to-handle parcel ready for trash pickup.

PLACEMENT AND CLEANING

Give some thought to the placement of the litter box. Many cats require privacy. If there is too much traffic where the litter box is located, the cat may decide it is safer to go elsewhere. Some cats like the covered litter boxes for this reason, but because odors may be emphasized inside covered boxes, you will have to be especially careful to keep these boxes clean.

Many cat owners do not realize that the cleaning materials they use to cleanse and deodorize the litter box might also repel the cat. Some cleaning products may even be dangerous to your cat's health. No matter what you use, rinse the pan thoroughly. To get rid of any offensive chlorine or ammonia odors that may be left behind, add baking soda to the rinse water and allow it to remain in the litter box for a few minutes.

LITTER BOX FILLERS

There is a wide selection of litter box fillers on the market; experiment to find the one that best fits your needs. Clay litters are the most popular, but some cat owners prefer to use sand, and one breeder I know swears that shredded newspaper, changed daily, is the most efficient. Occasionally you will find a cat that prefers only one kind of litter and refuses to use any other. Indulge him and just be happy he uses the box.

You don't really have to train a cat to use a litter box. Indoor cats are naturally clean, and with a little guidance they will accept and use their litter pan with no problems. This is especially true if the kitten was raised by a conscientious mother. Burying their feces is instinctive for cats. It's a trait carried over from their wild ancestors who used this technique to help hide their dens from predators.

It's a good idea to keep the litter box close to the kitten's sleeping area for at least the first few weeks. During this training period, it is also helpful if you place a small amount of soiled litter back in the clean box to remind the kitten what the box is used for. But always keep the litter box clean. Even as a youngster, a cat is fastidious and may refuse to use badly soiled litter. An offensive litter box can cause a kitten to develop poor bathroom habits as he matures.

CLAW OR DECLAW

Your cat's claws are one of the most important parts of his body. They are unique in their construction. Claws are utilized as fighting tools and grooming aids. They give your cat a feeling of well-being when used for kneading. They are truly indispensable for your cat's very existence if he lives out-of-doors.

When your cat stretches his claws and scratches, his feeling of self-esteem and contentment rises. If his claws are clipped, he is still able to extend and retract them, and is not affected by the loss of a small amount of nail.

Many owners of cats that never go outside clip their pets nails as a weekly ritual. This along with adequate scratching posts and toys for the cat's pleasure and entertainment, will usually prevent destructive scratching in the home.

It's common for young cats to occasionally scratch on forbidden furniture. An air, or water spray usually stops this destruction after a few disciplinary sessions. But what do you do with a cat that is truly destructive? After all discipline has been used consistently and every effort made to halt the damage, you may decide to have your cat declawed.

Declawing your cat is a major decision and should not be taken lightly. Once the cat's claws are removed, he must be protected for the rest of his life. If allowed to slip outside, your cat will be in constant danger and almost defenseless. Declawing is a drastic step to take, however a majority of felines survive the operation and live long lives. If it comes to getting rid of your cat or having him declawed, I would recommend you have the cat declawed.

PART 4

Man and Cat Living, Loving, Coping

PEACOCK FEATHERS—A POPULAR TICKLER

Usually the first thing you see when you enter a building where a cat show is being held are rows of tables filled with products to help you care for and delight your cats. There are all kinds of climbing trees carpeted in various fabrics, litter boxes of every description (and, of course, a selection of litter materials for filling them), health items, foods, vitamins, toys, and a library of books and pamphlets telling you how best to use all these products.

While the products displayed vary with each show, it's a rare assortment that doesn't include at least one tall jar holding peacock feathers. These are usually prominently displayed so that the soft down of each feather undulates hypnotically as the customers circulate about the tables making their selections.

Why peacock feathers at a cat show? The idea is perfectly simple. They make beautiful, enjoyable toys that will amuse both you and your cats for hours, even years. They are also widely used during the exhibitions in the show ring.

As the judging begins, each cat is brought from one of the cages behind the judging table. The cat is examined, displayed, discussed and finally returned to its cage. Most of the cats are docile and agreeable while being examined.

Because of this relaxed attitude, he may not display the alert, attentive expression that tells the judge so much about the cat's beauty and personality.

To obtain this desired expression, after all the cats in each category have been examined and returned to their cages, some judges walk along the cages flicking a peacock feather invitingly across the bars. As the iridescent feathers ripple before them, the cats leap forward, each with one paw raised to catch the wispy plume. At that moment, the cat's ears become erect, his eyes blaze with concentration and his whole being becomes alert. For just a few seconds, the cat shows off his beauty to the fullest. That's what the judge wants to see.

While cat shows are interesting and a great spectator sport for any cat lover, it's not necessary to attend one to enjoy your own cat's reaction to this delightful toy. In fact, peacock feathers are available in most pet supply stores and pet departments of the larger chain stores. If you have an attic, you may even find one free, attached to one of Grandma's old hats. They make reasonably-priced, unusual gifts for anyone who owns and loves felines.

Cats love to play the game of "chase the feather." Of course, other feathers may be used, but no other feather has the pliable strength and playful flow of the peacock feather. One sniff of the plumage stirs in the cat an instinct of ancestral hunters in days long gone by.

As you hold the stalk and ripple the downy plume across the floor, every muscle and all his senses leap to attention. With total concentration few humans ever experience, he stalks, parries and attacks, only to fall back and prepare for yet another assault. The rules of the game vary with each sweep of the feather, and both cat and player can become obsessed with devising complicated strategies calculated to surprise and outdo the opponent.

For any special occasion, why not gather a few peacock feathers, tie them together with a pretty bow to make an attractive bouquet and give it to one of your cat-loving friends? The blue-green plumage is lovely when displayed alone, or used in a bouquet of winter flowers. Even the most lackluster arrangement comes alive with the addition of a peacock feather or two. Your friends will be delighted with this unusual gift and you will have spent little time, money or effort spreading that joy.

SPRAYING—A TERRITORIAL INSTINCT

Cats spray urine to mark their territory. The scent left by spraying informs other felines of their territorial possessions. Upon smelling the odor, other cats do not appear frightened or intimidated, merely informed.

Tom cats spray a heavy scent that everyone recognizes immediately by the overpowering urine odor. Occasionally a female or neutered male will also spray, but usually they mark territory by scratching or by rubbing their chins, foreheads or tails, which contain scent glands, over an object leaving a mild odor on it. Often, when the marking scent produces a mild or inoffensive odor, a second cat, after careful investigation, will aggressively superimpose his own scent over the area, thus claiming it for his own.

Outdoors territorial marking, even in a small area, becomes clearly defined by all the felines living in a neighborhood. If the area is very small, the instinctive need for territorial marking adjusts to the situation, allowing the various cats to coexist peacefully. Of course, arguments do occur, but cats become so sophisticated in marking, that often the same territory belongs to different felines at varying times of the day. That is, a well-worn path may be one cat's territory in the morning, a second cat's territory in the afternoon, and a third cat's exclusive property at night.

Indoor pets instinctively use the same procedure as their outdoor cousins. Observe your felines. One cat will sun himself in a specific place each morning. Another one will have afternoon privileges in the same desired location with no argument from the first occupant. Pathways through the house are also marked by each cat. Specific trails, which make no sense to the observing human, are carefully followed each time the cat moves about the area. Up, down, around and through, the animals follow invisible trails and markings in a pattern, which the cat's owners, if not knowledgeable, might consider weird and unexplainable.

INDOOR SPRAYING

An indoor cat, especially if confined in a small area, may occasionally try to expand his realm. Many times, this desire for realignment of boundry lines happens after several years of seemingly happy coexistence with companion cats. Of course, sparks fly and tempers explode as his territorial drive tortures his owners. Vocalizing, hair raising, slapping and chasing—all become armaments in the battle for territory. The companion cats, unable to defend themselves from this domination and finding it difficult to escape, may resort to soiling or shying away, and if not helped may even become reclusive. Yesterday's happy household suddenly becomes today's battleground.

The owners of these felines are mystified to find themselves in the middle of all this turmoil. They have not observed the subtle, overt signs of scrimmages to come. Loving each cat, they are torn at being forced to take sides in each unacceptable attack. To top it off, the same cats that used to be so clean are now soiling all over the house.

To realign his boundries, an unneutered, or possibly a neutered male, sprays urine in seemingly random spots over the area. The companion cats, exhausted, nervous, unhappy and unable to cope with the situation, cry for help by refusing to use the litter box and soiling the rugs.

ISOLATION FOR SPRAY TRAINING

What do you do with your cats when this situation occurs in your home? Your immediate recourse is to isolate the spraying cat. Discipline will not help; the animal's actions are dictated by nature. You are dealing with 2,000 years of instinctive behavior that your cats could not change if they wanted to. Isolating the offending male will solve some of your immediate problems. You will be able to clean and thoroughly deodorize your home. The other cats will be able to relax and hopefully resume their normal routine.

Many times, isolating the male in a small room or cage for several weeks helps him to forget, but this will usually help only if the male has been neutered. It is important that he be isolated continuously for several weeks. You can go into his area to feed, change the litter box and give the cat some affection, but don't allow him into the rest of the house.

Before you allow your cats to meet again, wipe each one with a solution of vinegar and water. Saturate their coats well to remove any offensive odors that might prompt renewed battles.

The first week when you bring the male cat into the family area, isolate the other cats for the few hours he is with you. It will be enough for him to readjust to the area alone without the other cats around. While playing with him and allowing him to roam about, you should have available a spray bottle filled with vinegar and water. Hopefully, the previously soiled areas are now odorless and the cat will ignore them. If by chance, he starts to soil, you must be ready to give him a spray of water in the face, together with a firm "No!" command.

Over the next few weeks, you can continue allowing your aggressive boy access to the household areas frequently and for longer intervals. Take your time with this retraining, and you may succeed once and for all. Reintroduce his former companions when you feel all cats are ready to meet. If you are doing well, but the disciplined cat suddenly relapses into his previously bad behavior, isolate him again and start over. Don't be discouraged; it shouldn't take as long the second time around.

Many times veterinarians prescribe hormones to try to alleviate the spraying problem. Sometimes hormone injections are successful, but often the medication doesn't work. If your retraining efforts don't obtain the desired results, consult your vet.

INTRODUCING SECOND CAT IS TOUCHY

Much to my surprise, a friend who had found a stray cat at a local market, walked into my house and set the cat down. Fortunately for all involved, the cat immediately seemed at ease with our household pets. They, though curious, did nothing worse than run into the kitchen to guard their food.

Baby, as we called him, leaving a proper name to the future owner, turned out to be a gentle, loving boy, apparently about 5 months old. He had big paws and a large bone structure, indicating that he was destined to become a very impressive adult. We enjoyed having the cat around us and he had such winning ways we were sorely tempted to add him to our menagerie. Fortunately the next day we received a telephone call for help that established Baby's future home.

Paul and Judy were having discipline problems with their one-year-old Siamese male, named Sammy. He had always been temperamental and high-strung, but as he got older, he became snippy, and at times downright mean.

His over-indulgent owners had tried once before to bring a small kitten into their home as a companion for Sammy. Their effort had failed, partly because the meeting was not well planned and partly because they had introduced a young defenseless kitten to a large, strong-willed dictator. The kitten was soon rescued and given to another home.

Paul and Judy, reluctant to go through another nerve-wracking encounter, had asked me to help them find a proper companion for Sammy to work off some of his excess energy. Meanwhile, at my suggestion, Sammy was being neutered.

Baby was certainly the perfect size and had the right disposition to adjust to their temperamental cat; but I knew that Sammy would not accept another feline in his home without thoughtful advance preparation.

Since Sammy had definitely established territorial rights to every room in his home, I decided that we should introduce the cats in neutral territory. Our home seemed the only sensible place, so we arranged an evening for the meeting. I have helped introduce a second cat quite a few times, and it is always a touchy situation. Often you do not have a second chance once the territorial cat rejects the invader.

In preparation for the cats' meeting, I asked my son to wipe Sammy down with a solution of apple cider vinegar and water. After drying, he had to be sprinkled with baby powder. Baby received the same treatment at our home. With this precaution, both cats would lose their specific body odors and smell familiarly alike.

On the appointed evening, I placed our other household pets in a comfortable upstairs bedroom so they could not complicate matters.

As Sammy came through the door in his owner's arms, he was yelling his Siamese disapproval. When placed on the floor, he became mollified and sniffed the carpet and furniture. Advancing halfway across the living room, Sammy was suddenly confronted by Baby, casually entering through the kitchen doorway.

One look and Sam dropped to a crouch, each hair on his body soaring to attention. As Sammy bellied threateningly across the floor toward the kitten, Baby circled in the opposite direction, each approaching the other from the rear.

Once within nose reach, Sammy stretched his neck to smell his rival. Baby backed away each time Sam's nose came near. Persistently, Sammy tried to smell Baby's tail until finally our good-natured boy, tired of retreating, smacked Sammy, ran across the room and jumped upon the seat of a chair. Sammy's hair slowly flattened as he stood up, walked to the chair and batted Baby's draping tail. Since there was no offensive odor and no difference in smell, the cats began a hesitantly playful chase around the room.

The cats' first encounter lasted for two hours. Each was cautious while playing, never really trusting the other. Sammy, confused and fearful, had behaved better than we had hoped; but he was a long way from accepting Baby as a lasting friend.

Paul and Judy were encouraged by Sammy's less aggressive behavior and carefully followed our plan. For the next two evenings, both cats were wiped all over with the vinegar and water mixture followed by powder, and reunited.

During the cats' second meeting, Sammy was excited and eager to find Baby as he jumped from his owner's arms and sashayed across the room. Baby, delighted to see his new friend, smacked Sammy across the head. The chase was on.

That evening and the following night were very different from the cats' first meeting. Now they romped, bit and scratched each other, playing gently but more aggressively each time they met. While they rested between bouts, we could hear them talking to each other in soft gutteral purrs.

On the fourth night, it was decided that the cats were ready to live together. Sammy had used Baby's litter box occasionally while he was visiting, and he had even eaten out of Baby's food dish. In other words, Sammy had established himself as top cat and Baby seemed agreeable to the arrangement most of the time.

As our daughter-in-law related later, there was little sleep for either humans or cats that first night at home. Sammy had always shared his king-size bed with his owners; but he spent half the night chasing Baby away. Baby, though not as clever as Sam, was just as persistent and kept coming back for more. By 4:00 in the morning, both cats, too exhausted to continue, curled up with Paul and Judy and fell asleep.

During the next few weeks, Sammy, Baby and their owners slowly adjusted to their new living arrangement. Whenever the cats got huffy with each other, potential battles were avoided by powdering both cats again.

Sammy has a long way to go before he relaxes completely with another cat in the house. Maybe he will always be highstrung and excitable. At least, we know Sam is happier sharing his lonely hours with Baby than being alone and Paul and Judy no longer feel guilty leaving their cats at home while they work or take a day for pleasure.

Most of all, although no one thought of it but me, my Baby had a wonderful, loving home. That's my reward.

GROWING OLD, FEELING GOOD

Old age comes all too soon for our beloved family pets. Yet of the three stages of life—youth, maturity and old age—the last can be the most rewarding.

113

By the time a cat is ten years old, signs of aging appear. The once sparkling eyes lose their luster; hair becomes thinner and lacks the shine that constant grooming makes possible. Your old tiger is no longer jumping, playing and demanding attention as he did in his prime.

In fact, he is now content to spend his time sleeping and taking short walks around the house and yard. The cat accepts and enjoys the attention you give, then lounges away the hours in his favorite spot watching the rest of the world whirl around.

Your cat's golden years can and should be a wonderful experience for both of you. While it is necessary to stay alert for signs of physical and psychological complications, a majority of healthy, well-cared-for felines proceed through their teen years with good health and an astonishing amount of vigor. It's best to continue with your cat's daily routine as he ages, unless you notice changes that indicate discomfort or irritability.

LITTER BOX DISORDERS—OLDER CATS

Many times your senior citizen will show physical or mental stress by refusing to use his litter pan, or worse, insulting you by soiling right beside it. If this happens after years of cleanliness, you should look for the source of your cat's problem. Few cats will indiscriminately soil without justifiable cause. Of course, you and your pet may have a differing definition of "justifiable cause," especially in this frustrating situation.

Many times, the most simple motive is the explanation:

HAS YOUR DAILY routine been changed, thus causing

your cat emotional stress? A good example of this is a change from daytime to nighttime work among the family members. Have you accepted a job requiring long hours away from home, when your cat has always had your daily companionship? You can overcome these problems; but you must remember your old cat loves a never-changing schedule. Perhaps you can give your pet a little more affection when you come home and during your after-work activities. With these small efforts, the cat will eventually re-adjust his schedule and return to his former cleanliness. During this adjustment period, you should express your disapproval over his litter box behavior.

DID YOU MOVE your cat's litter box to a different area? If so, put it back and slowly move the box a little each day until you have the litter where you want it. If kitty objects, you'll have to figure out a compromise, if possible. At least, there is one simple solution: move the box back to its original place. Then, thank your lucky stars your cat is once again clean.

DO YOU HAVE a new tenant in your home? Be it man, woman, dog, baby or another cat, your old boy will not share your enthusiasm for the intruder. Proper introduction to the stranger will help; but you, the one your cat focuses his affection on, must take the time to help your distressed senior citizen to adjust.

Many feline owners, out of affection for their old friend, bring a kitten into the home thinking their cat will be happier. This is a misconception and should not be believed. Even though life seems boring for the elderly pet, he is content with his routine and should be allowed to monopolize your attention as long as possible. Of course, there are changes in your lifestyle that he must accept; but unless the older cat adopts another kitten or cat of his own free will, you will both be happier leaving your home life as it is.

DID A MEMBER of the family leave home? The death or departure of a companion causes great stress in the elderly cat. He must learn to adjust; but you can help by giving more attention and affection to your old buddy during this difficult period.

ARE PHYSICAL REASONS preventing your cat from using his litter box? Is he having pain during urination? Is he straining when he attempts to evacuate? He may be telling you of his distress by bringing attention to his litter box misbehavior. A trip to the veterinarian for a diagnosis should be made as soon as possible.

IS YOUR CAT feeling discomfort when going up and down the stairs? This could be a simple answer, if you have always put the litter box in the basement, or in an upstairs bath or bedroom. Perhaps your cat has painful arthritis and no longer wants to climb as he used to. Putting the litter box, along with his food dishes and bed in the living area he shares with you, may bring peace and cleanliness once more.

If you notice stiffness or pain when your cat moves, you can add to his comfort by placing a stool, ladder or chair under the high areas he has always enjoyed. Aging bones may not respond to jumping to the high places that were accessible when he was young. These aids will allow your old boy to continue, with dignity, to enjoy the daily pleasures he relishes so dearly.

PREVENTIVE MEDICINE FOR ELDERLY CATS

Preventive medicine is most important for assuring your cat a comfortable, healthy old age. Yearly checkups should be stressed as the feline ages and all booster shots should be scheduled when necessary.

OLDER CATS DO not require as much food as they did in younger days; and being overweight is a serious drawback to good health. As the elderly, less active cat gains weight, the fat stored in his system requires more energy to make the vital organs function. This causes an additional burden to the heart, kidneys and digestive system. The most common geriatric problems are kidney disorders, tumors, arthritis and heart conditions. Obesity can be a major detriment in most of these occurrences.

LOSS OF APPETITE is a frequent occurrence at one time or another as your cat ages. Certainly the sense of smell and taste are decreasing over the years. Many times stronger flavoring added to your pet's food will stimulate the appetite. Garlic, onion and fish flavorings are especially enticing to a fussy feline and, of course, mixed meat, vegetables, butter and fats encourage lagging appetites.

Along with the declining appetite, tartar build-up on your cat's teeth may cause eating discomfort. It may be directly related to loss of appetite, since excessive tartar can cause gum infections. This results in loose, and eventually, lost teeth. Eating then becomes very painful. You should inspect your cat's teeth occasionally for tartar and receeding gums.

A weekly routine of wiping the teeth with a piece of rough toweling will help. If the condition becomes severe, a veterinarian will have to put your cat temporarily to sleep and give his teeth a thorough scraping. Fortunately, tartar removal doesn't need to be repeated very often.

GOOD GROOMING OR looking good surely must be the first requirement for admittance into cat heaven. This must be true since all healthy felines spend hours each day washing their coats to shining perfection. A well-groomed coat is the sign of a healthy cat. Grooming gives him exercise, a feeling of well-being, and helps to work off excess energy.

MUTUAL GROOMING IS the ultimate affection shown by companion cats. For aging cats, grooming can become an overwhelming burden. Even though they try to maintain their coats, the extra energy required is not there. If this happens to your old pal, it's time for you to step in and help with this daily chore. When you groom your cat, you are showing affection and re-establishing his feeling of well-being. This is important to the feline's mental health. All experts agree that helping your pet look and feel well-groomed increases his life expectancy.

OCCASIONALLY THE AGING CAT must have a bath. Frequent spot washing around his face, ears and tail will help maintain cleanliness, but there does come a time when a warm water bath must be given to make the cat smell nice again. If you are hesitant about bathing him, many grooming shops now include this as an added service.

When spot washing and brushing your pet, watch for lumps, warts and beginning mats. Malignant lumps or tumors can be successfully treated, if discovered early. Mats found when they are just forming can be easily sprayed with "mat and tangle remover" or oil and gently pulled apart by your fingers with no discomfort to your pet.

DEATH AND DYING

Death and dying eventually come to all living creatures, but your aged cat will suffer less than you. The decision to put an end to your pet's suffering is made with know-

118

ledge and love. You need not make this difficult decision alone. Your veterinarian will be most helpful in consultation about the health of your family pet.

The decision to put him to sleep is not a single problem. It must be discussed with the entire family and ultimately decided by all involved. Although painful for the family, the final act of love—relieving your old friend of pain and suffering—is the merciful decision you must inevitably make. Many owners of aging cats delay this difficult step too long. When the proper time arrives, euthanasia is suggested.

If you feel, however, that your pet is still enjoying life relatively free from pain, take each day as it comes and delay the end by giving him good care and affection. If you love your pet, show the strength necessary to consider him first.

CHRISTMAS SAFETY

Each holiday its fun to find suggestions for seasonal gifts. I offer an assortment of ideas for seasonal gifts to make for cats. It also makes me feel better when I include some holiday home safety suggestions. I don't want you to think that these ideas come from some divine revelation, or like a bolt out of the blue. The truth is, they come from years of learning about cats the hard way—through trial and error.

Our family has owned cats that disdainfully ignored our Christmas trees. We have even owned a few cats that angelically sat before the decorated tree, watching the blinking lights while patiently waiting for their gifts. Most of our curious felines, however, have to our dismay, climbed our beautifully decorated trees, and cats and trees came tumbling down.

Finally through the years, we've worked out a sure-fire system which insures both a house safe from cat damage, and most importantly, a cat having fun while enjoying a safe holiday season.

SECURING THE TREE

Each year before we place our Christmas tree in front of the living room window, one of the family members climbs a ladder and screws two small metal eyes into the top surface of the window frame. We put the eyes about a foot to each side of where the center of the tree will stand. From each eye, a strong thin wire is secured, then brought forward and tied to the upper trunk of the tree. The metal eyes in the molding and the wires to the tree are virtually impossible to see once the tree is decorated. If we have a smaller tree, we adjust the wires until satisfied that the tree will remain upright—even if our latest cat decides to climb the inviting new toy.

Once our Christmas tree is secured in its floor holder and fastened with wires from above, the strings of electric lights are brought from the attic. The lights are then laid out around the living room floor and checked for burned out bulbs and dangerously exposed wiring. While the lights are strung around the room, I walk about and place dabs of Tabasco sauce on portions of the wires, particularly the bit of wire that runs along the floor between the last light bulb and the wall outlet. Tabasco sauce will not harm animals, but its hot taste will discourage cats from chewing on the dangerous wires.

After all the preliminary work is done, the fun begins as we start decorating the tree. Years ago we decided it was sensible to place the precious older family bulbs, as well as any edible decorations, in the upper half of the branches. Along the very lowest branches are hung playful, attractive plastic toys, harmless to sniffs and swats from our curious feline companions.

When the tree is finally decorated, our last job is to fill the water pan beneath the tree. After the tree is watered, the festive tree skirt is tightly tied to the trunk of the tree above the water. To reinforce the skirt ties, a bit of wire is also wound around the tree trunk over the skirt ties. This prevents household pets from drinking the tainted water.

At the same time we were working out all the necessities to ensure our family and cats a safe holiday, we discovered a delightful toy to keep our cats occupied during the festivities. Quite by accident we found that a box containing a catnip mouse can become a source of entertainment.

Two weeks before Christmas, one of our children, with childish delight, wrapped a box containing a catnip mouse in gay holiday paper and placed the present under the tree. The cats were excited. The smell of delicious catnip was enticingly out of reach inside the box. The rattle of cellophane within the lightweight parcel piqued their curiosity. The gift became an amusing favorite toy before it was opened! The cats pushed, tossed and fought playfully until the grand opening on Christmas Eve. Each year we have continued to present this gift, and all our cats have found hours of amusement from one child's loving thoughtfulness.

GIFTS CHILDREN CAN MAKE

All children enjoy making gifts long before their small fingers can manipulate scissors and tools. Since cats enjoy playing in paper bags, here is a simple, inexpensive present to make for grandmother's or uncle's favorite cat.

Purchase some wide colored tape for sealing packages. If you cannot find a color, wide brown masking tape will work just as well. Using the largest and strongest grocery bag you can find, help your child cut a three-inch square hole in the center of one of the wide sides. Reinforce the edge of the hole and all folds of the bag with the colored tape. Also reinforce the top edge of the bag to help the paper resist tearing. You now have a colorful bag in which

122

any cat will love to hide. The hole in the side of the bag will entice your pet to reach out to catch your fingers when you play with him.

The bag may be further decorated any way your imaginative child wishes. My young son simply used red tape on the brown bag and blocked in red felt pen, the words "CAT HOLE" with an arrow pointing to the spot. This toy was attractive and both relatives and cats loved the gift.

Ping pong balls are a cat's delight—lightweight, durable and as full of bounce as the pet that plays with them. Most important of all, ping pong balls make creative, inexpensive gifts. Give your child some scissors, scraps of material, felt, colored markers or crayons, and let his or her imagination soar to the heights. Ask your child, "What do you see when you hold the round white ball?" Glue on two ears, draw eyes, a nose and whiskers—why it's a cat! "Can you make a mouse? I'm sure Tabby will love it as much as Grandma will."

Wicker baskets for pet beds are an "in" item this season. They are attractive, comfortable, but expensive. Since all young animals will chew on wicker, before you give a wicker bed as a gift, or if you have received or bought a wicker bed, I hope you'll take a few minutes to insure your pet's safety with these inexpensive precautions.

Wash and dry a pair of old nylon stockings. Tie one stocking leg neatly at the corner of the basket opening. Spread the nylon out as you wrap the material in, out, and around the wicker opening. When one stocking comes to an end, overlap another nylon, secure it and keep wrapping until the wicker is covered. Nylon stockings are also effective when used to wrap plastic or vinyl cat beds.

Take some extra time and follow these safety procedures. It's better to be safe than sorry.

PART 5

Questions
and
Answers

Questions

&

Answers

OLDER CAT, NEW KITTEN ADJUSTMENT

Q *I just got a new kitten and my older cat refuses to like him. I have heard and read that cats should learn to coexist with each other in a week or less. Well, it's been more than a week and now whenever the kitten or I get near the adult cat, she scratches us. Do you have any suggestions to help get rid of this situation?*

A Your adult cat feels that you and the kitten are leaving her out of all the fun. I know it's hard to ignore a kitten, but that's what you're going to have to do for awhile. When you ignore the kitten and pay more attention to the adult cat, the cats will work out a living arrangement together. (Without your attention, the kitten will turn to the older cat for companionship.) Once your older cat becomes friendly with the kitten, it will be up to you to see that they both get an equal amount of attention. In fact, the older cat will probably demand, and get, a bigger share, and little brother won't even notice.

DEAF CAT BECOMES NEUROTIC

Q *For the last year, my neutered, male, white Persian, who is deaf, has been acting mean, hissing for no reason and running off, scared. He is six years old and I've had him since he was a baby.*

Last October I brought home a nine-week-old female sealpoint Himalayan kitten. After a year the two tolerate each other, but that's about all. I keep them separate at night when we are not home and give them each their own dish and litter box.

Last March they both had tapeworm and the Persian could not get enough to eat. They were both treated and started gaining weight. Now he weighs 13 pounds and has an obsession with food. The only time he is friendly any more is when I'm eating and he wants some.

Lately, he will be sitting calmly by himself and all of a sudden his ears go back and he looks around as if scared, he'll hiss, run off and cower. He did this four times in a row the other day while I was at the kitchen table eating. Nobody bothered him to cause this, not even the Himalayan. I'd appreciate any advice you could give me. He doesn't act sick and I hate to get rid of him.

A After much thought and worry about your problem, I consulted a few of my cat associates, and they confirmed my opinion. You have a problem which you cannot solve.

128

Apparently your older, deaf Persian cannot adjust to sharing his home and loved ones. He is becoming extremely neurotic, and the only answer, for your peace of mind, is to find a good home for one of the cats. Since you assure me that the cats have no physical problems, you must assume that your deaf cat will not change and proceed from there. Good luck.

OLD ODOR ON CARPET

Q *We have just moved into a nice home in Illinois. The only problem that we have is a smelly carpet from the previous owner's cat. How can we remove the odor without paying for professional services?*

A Cat urine does seem to smell stronger with age and the odor is both unpleasant and frustrating to get rid of. The best method I have ever used to remove both stains and odor takes little time, effort or money. It is very effective.

You will need a large bottle of soda water (as in scotch and soda) and a large number of paper towels, paper napkins or facial tissues. Pour one cup of soda water on each soiled area, soaking it well. Let the soda water stand for 20 to 30 minutes. If the spot is old or very soiled, rub the area well with a rough sponge or brush. Blot the carpet dry with the absorbent paper. It is very important that you keep changing the blotting paper until all moisture is absorbed. You will then be sure that you have removed all of the dirt and odor broken down by the soda water. Repeat this process if necessary after the rug has completely dried. If you have brought another pet into the home, sprinkle pepper on the dry rug to discourage any further use. As an added precaution, spray the previously soiled area with a good deodorizer, such as Nilodor.

SOGGY RUGS

Q *I have five cats that stay indoors since we live by a busy street. My problem with three of them is they urinate on throw rugs, but not the laid carpet. I can't put any rug down without them leaving their mark. The cats are male neuters. Are they just lazy cats, or are they telling me something with their behavior? Can anything be done to stop this behavior?*

A Your cats' poor behavior may result from boredom, a dirty litter box or simply one cat started soiling and the rest followed suit. I'm sure you have thought of all these reasons and have provided toys, scratching post, etc. to entertain your felines. What many cat owners do not realize is that once a pet soils a rug, the odor goes deep into the carpet, the padding, and even the flooring below. The smell will lure the cat back to the same spot. Washing the rug is not enough. Remove the throw rugs you've been using, and either throw them away or wash and deodorize them and put them aside for a few months.

Don't be surprised if your cats still insist on soiling the same areas, even though the rugs have been removed. After you have removed the rugs, it will be necessary to thoroughly clean and deodorize the floor beneath. There are many good products on the market made especially to remove urine odor, or you can use your own household cleaner. With wood flooring, be particularly careful to clean the cracks. During the next two months, clean the floor several times to permanently remove the odor. As an extra deterrent, you can place a chair or any piece of furniture upside down over each previously used spot to prevent the cats from soiling again during the cleanup process. You really will have no trouble correcting this situation if you deodorize carefully.

As a final precaution, I like to put a little pepper, vinegar or tabasco sauce on the forbidden spots. It's also good to use the repellents on the rugs when they are placed on the floor again.

HOSPITAL ODORS CONFUSE COMPANION CATS

Q   *Recently, I had a battle of dominance between my two cats. Both are city apartment cats who live with me alone in a small apartment with no access to the out-of-doors.*

My 15-year-old female Siamese, Thai, underwent dental surgery and came home the same day, weak and groggy. Over the next three days, my four-year-old male hybrid, Tigger, showed the most bizarre and unaccustomed behavior. He repeatedly attacked Thai, growling and bristling. No damage was done, but she was alarmed and frightened, and so was I.

My vet suggested that the cats were fighting for the position of "top cat" in the household. I was advised to let my younger cat know his behavior was unacceptable. It took about a week before he finally returned to his old, sweet self, and the problem has not recurred. It was almost impossible for me to separate them, so I never did.

My problem is that Thai, although in relatively good health, will probably continue to have health problems as she ages. What do I do about protecting her and solving the dominance problem? Will Tigger get more aggressive as she weakens? I would appreciate your advice and wonder what others do in such a situation.

A In multi-cat households, it is usually true that there is one cat who is dominant over the household or some particular area within the household. This dominance varies from absolute tyranny to benevolent dictatorship. Usually the oldest or first resident becomes dominant, regardless of sex. The bizarre behavior displayed by your younger cat doesn't necessarily mean he was battling for control over your older cat. In fact, your young cat would have a hard time getting the upper hand on any healthy 15-year-old. From a strong-willed, people-loving Siamese, like your Thai, it would be almost impossible.

There is no question that Tigger was upset and confused when he attacked his old friend Thai with what, to you, seemed little or no provocation. I'm pretty sure what actually happened was that poor old Thai came home smelling like a veterinary hospital and Tigger couldn't believe that any cat smelling like an animal hospital could be his old roommate. He then acted as he would toward any strange cat that invaded his home.

After a few days in the apartment, Thai had washed and rubbed off most of the obnoxious odor (which she hated as much as Tigger) and all was well again. Tigger realized his mistake when Thai began smelling like the pal he knew and loved, and peace reigned again in your home.

Many cat owners fail to understand that felines, whether living in the wild or in a home, use their sense of smell over all other senses. Feline olfactory systems are highly developed and rarely fail to identify individual scents. Since hospital odors such as antiseptics are pungent and remain in animal hair for several days, pet owners upon bringing their pets home, should neutralize all odor in the fur by giving their pet a bath. Many times a firm rub with a towel soaked in vinegar/water solution will be more acceptable to the animal and also prevent chilling if the pet is aged or ill.

As to future problems with your aging cat, it is best to just face each problem as it comes. As the years go by give Thai protection, if necessary, lots of love and preventive health care. Since your cats are usually loving with each other, I doubt that Tigger will attack again if you wash Thai's fur after each hospital visit. In fact it's not a bad idea to wash down both cats so they will smell alike.

Surprisingly, while most pet owners are not familiar with this problem, cat breeders encounter this hostility between their cats frequently. At the last show, one breeder told me, "When I notice my cats starting to bicker and fuss, I usually powder them all down with a little baby powder. It's a simple system, but the cats seem to settle down and enjoy each other again."

MEDICATE FOR ANXIETY ATTACKS

Q *We have a beautiful, 2-year-old male cat which we acquired as a stray. We love him dearly, except for one annoying habit we cannot seem to break him of: biting. Whenever we pet him, he will sit for a few seconds and then begin to bite—hard. We had him neutered, hoping that would help, but it didn't. We know he was abused* *before he came to us. Could this have anything to do with it? Do you have any suggestions?*

A Your cat was certainly lucky to find such understanding owners, because he is going to need all of the help your loving family can give him. There is no doubt that your cat is suffering from anxiety and stress. Cats who have been abused or who have lacked affection while they grew cannot help but suffer later in life. It will take patience on your part to help your cat establish a good self-image and learn to relax and enjoy life.

For a while, resist the temptation to pick up the cat except when necessary. If he jumps on your lap, talk to him but don't pet or scratch him. Talk to your cat as often as you can. Use his name and speak lovingly and quietly. If you wish, lean down and pet his head or scratch his ears, but only for a moment at a time. When your cat does lie down with you, stay calm, take deep breaths and allow him to feel how relaxed you are. This will relieve some of his anxiety. If you study the cat's behavior, you will find there are certain body movements that precede each attack. When you see or feel your cat tense for the attack, get up and leave before the cat carries out the action.

I think your cat would also benefit from a mild tranquilizer given daily for a few months. As his anxieties lessen, you can taper off the medication. Talk to your veterinarian about this and start as soon as possible. Your cat is young and will no doubt be the delight of your life as soon as his problems are solved.

HITTING—INEFFECTIVE DISCIPLINE

Q *I have a two and a half year old, female, half tabby and half Siamese cat. She is not an affectionate cat and seldom enjoys being held. My problem is this: When I try to pet her, she will either respond by rolling on her back, or she will bite me viciously. On other occasions she attacks and bites my ankles. I say no and she'll do it again, harder and harder. I will then hit her on the rear and she will viciously bite me as hard as she possibly can and walk away. In the same situation, I will put her out of the room and close the door. After a few minutes she will cry and I'll open the door. Generally, her biting will cease.*

Help, I can't stand her biting. I'm all scarred up. How can I stop her vicious attacks?

A I am firmly convinced that hitting a cat on the back end is ineffective and leads to retaliation. In other words, the cat will find some way of paying you back. I suggest that you carry a spray bottle of water around with you and when the silent stalker attacks, shoot a full spray of water in her face. As soon as the cat stops biting, lean down and pet her to reinforce her good behavior.

Cats will often bite or grab the hand that scratches their tummy, as they roll around on their back. Many times the biting is from pleasure instead of anger. Regardless of the reason, it is painful and the cat must cease. A snap on the cat's nose will shock the cat and stop the attack. Once again, always give affection for good behavior.

STOP CAT DIGGING

Q *I have a cat that is a year old. She is declawed because she is an inside cat and she plays with my dog all the time.*

I go to school. My mother works during the day, and so does my father. Every day when I get home, my mother's plants are all dug up. Even when I go on vacation she digs up all of our plants. I scold her, but she keeps on doing it. Why does she do it? Is there anything I can do to stop her?

A Your cat sounds normal and very nice, except for her digging problem. If you and I can figure out how to stop your cat's bad habit, all will be happy in your house again. Try this! Ask mom to buy some Tabasco sauce at the grocery store. Tabasco, a hot sauce to put into chili or Mexican dishes tastes hot, but it will not hurt your cat. Put dabs of Tabasco on the rim of the flower pots and some on the dirt. Your mother can help if you need it. Another good repellent is red or black pepper sprinkled in the dirt.

While you are keeping the cat away from the plants, remember that she is probably digging out of boredom. Be sure to give your cat some toys to play with while you are away.

TRAFFIC DANGER TO OUTDOOR CAT

Q *We live in a suburban town in New Jersey. Our alley cat named Suzie was a healthy indoor-outdoor cat. She* *was six years old in March when she died. We think she was hit by a car. Suzie's spinal cord was broken, and we had to have her put to sleep. It was very sad. We would like to get another cat and train it not to go into the street. I think cats have a right to go in and out as they please, but I would like to train the cat to protect itself. Thank you for your help.*

A Sorry, I wish I could find a magic solution to this impossible problem, but there is none.

Cats can learn a great deal through patient training by their handlers and owners; but I have never heard of a cat successfully trained to avoid streets. Cats also learn from experience, but often the price they pay for their experience is too high. Pet ownership always involves a certain amount of worry and concern, but allowing a cat to roam freely near busy streets is inviting disaster. Cats can live long, healthy and happy lives indoors. Perhaps you can train yourself to accept that lifestyle for your cat!

DISORIENTED CAT

Q *We moved into a new mobile home recently. Our six-year-old cat suddenly refused to use his litter box and started using the register in the dining room. Needless to say, we are not happy with the old boy's behavior. Can you help us figure him out?*

A Your old boy is probably suffering from displacement shock. Cats don't like to have their life patterns changed. First, try giving the cat lots of affection. At the same time, clean the heating duct and thoroughly deodorize the whole area. You can probably find a cake deodorant, made for toilets, that will hang below the register grill (inaccessible to the cat) and act as a repellent. Now fix a nice, clean litter box far away from the dining room and watch the cat for a few days to be sure he understands that he must follow the house rules. Good luck!

SHY CAT MAY BE HAPPY

Q *I have a shy cat two and a half years old. My Angela has progressed but I would like some more ideas on how to help her.*

If I am alone, Angela will come to me and curl up in my lap to be petted and loved, but even the presence of another family member makes her hide and refuse to make an appearance. Sometimes I have wondered if the agony she lives with of being frightened all of the time is worth it for her. Yet, when we are alone, it is hard to believe she is the same cat.

Do you or any readers have ideas on how I can help her out of her shyness and the misery of confronting other people?

A Angela does sound unusually shy, and possibly a little disturbed. However, you have been working on her problems for two and a half years with some results. Certainly, you are doing everything possible to make life comfortable and easy for your cat; so I think you should relax, accept and enjoy your devoted friend. It sounds as if you are

138

fighting basic instincts which are sometimes impossible to battle.

Many cats live in isolation with ill or handicapped people for years and are absolutely content. In fact, our family also owned a shy cat that spent all of her time in a bedroom, unless her owner (my daughter) was at home. Looking back, I still believe that our "shy cat" was simply a one-person feline and lived a perfectly happy life.

Jerry Climer also offers special interest articles for $2.00 per subject, or three for $5.00.

Subjects:

A. How to start an animal shelter

B. How to make an attractive shoulder strap cat carrier

C. Teaching your cat to use a cat door

D. Home furnishings for you and your pet.

How to RAISE A DOG

when nobody's home!

By
JERRY CLIMER

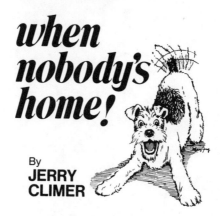

HOW TO RAISE A DOG WHEN NOBODY'S HOME is also available from your local bookstore, or it may be ordered for the same price as HOW TO RAISE A CAT WHEN NOBODY'S HOME from

Penny Dreadful Publishers
P.O. Box 364
Jackson, Michigan 49204